HOW I WAS GUIDED TO TAWHID AND THE STRAIGHT PATH

A Translation Of

Kayfa Ihtadaytū Īlā At-Tawhīd Wa Ṣirāt Al-Mustaqīm

By Shaykh Muḥammad b. Jamīl Zeno

Translated, Edited And Annotated By Abū Ubaydah Arsalān Yūnus

Ark of Knowledge
PUBLICATIONS

How I Was Guided To *Tawhīd* And The Straight Path
(Kayfa Ihtadaytū Īlā At-Tawhīd Wa Ṣirāt Al-Mustaqīm)
First Edition
Published by Ark Of Knowledge Publications, Leeds
info@aokpubs.com
www.aokpubs.com

ISBN: 9798872821267

Contents

FOREWORD

I begin with every beautiful name that belongs to *Allāh*, the Most Gracious, the Most Merciful.

All complete praise is due to *Allāh* alone the *Rabb*[1] of all that exists. May blessings and greetings of peace be upon the best of His creation Muḥammad (صلى الله عليه وسلم), the last and final Messenger, and upon his family, companions and all those who follow him until the day of Judgement.

This is a comprehensive translation of the book *Kayfa Ihtadaytū Īlā At-Tawhīd Wa Ṣirāt Al-Mustaqīm*, How I Was Guided To *Tawhīd* And The Straight Path, by the esteemed scholar Shaykh Muḥammad b. Jamīl Zeno.

This book is the autobiography of the famous Arab scholar Muḥammad b. Jamīl Zeno, who responded to a request from a Turkish student of knowledge that wanted to know more about the Shaykh's life.

It is a completely different and unique memoire compared to the common stories. Shaykh Muḥammad b. Jamīl Zeno has embellished his narrative with the beauty of strong and irrefutable arguments from the *Qur'ān* and *Sunnah* so that every reader can be completely satisfied with his rationalisation.

The story of the Shaykh's life is written in such an interesting way that the reader gets lost in it to the extent that he feels as though he is traveling with the Shaykh himself to different places.

Some beneficial footnotes compiled by me are marked as translator's notes [TN] to further aid the readers in their pursuit of seeking the reality of this topic.

Although every effort has been made to ensure this modern translation is as accurate as possible, if there are any obvious errors in it, then I will be deeply grateful to its readers to provide feedback and guidance.

I hope that this book benefits others. If so, then it is only a blessing from *Allāh*, and then the product of guidance from my teachers and encouragement of sincere friends. I also hope that with works like this, I can make a modest contribution to the right

1 [TN] The word *Rabb* has a vast meaning. Its detailed meaning is the Sustainer, Cherisher, Master and Nourisher.

understanding of *Islām*. I sincerely ask *Allāh* to accept my meagre efforts in this regard.

I ask *Allāh* to make this simple endeavour a source of pleasure for us all and a source of success in the Hereafter. *Āmīn*

Abū Ubaydah Arsalān Yūnus
Rabi Uth-Thānī, 1445 *Hijrī*

INTRODUCTION

Indeed all complete praise belongs to *Allāh* alone, we praise Him, seek His help and seek His forgiveness. We seek refuge with *Allāh* from the evil of our own selves and our own evil actions. Whomsoever *Allāh* guides then no one can misguide him and whomsoever *Allāh* misguides then no one can guide him. I testify that there is no deity worthy of worship in truth except *Allāh* alone, who has no partners. I also testify that Muḥammad (صلى الله عليه وسلم) is His slave and Messenger.

To proceed, I received a letter from a Turkish student from the city of Konya [in Turkey]. The text of it was,

To Muḥammad b. Jamīl Zeno, the teacher in *Dār al-Ḥadīth al-Khayriyyah* at *Makkah al-Mukarramah.*

Asalāmū 'Alaykum Wa Rahmatullāhī Wa Barakatuh

Our Noble teacher, I am a student of knowledge in the faculty of *Sharī'ah* at Konya. I took your book, *'The Islāmic Belief'* and translated it into Turkish as part of my thesis but I require your biography so that I can include it within the publication. I require that you send me these details please at the following address. Thank you for now, and may peace be upon those who follow the guidance.[2]

Bilal Baromaji

Many other students of knowledge have requested me to write about the story of my life and the various stages that I traversed since I was younger till I reached around 70 years old, and how I was guided towards the correct *Islāmic* belief of the righteous predecessors, based on the evidences from the Noble *Qur'ān* and the *Ṣahīh Aḥadīth.* This is a great blessing and no one knows this except the one who tasted it.

---

[2] The *Salām* and greeting in this form is not permissible to state to a Muslim. Rather it is for the non-Muslims who do not follow the guidance. As for the *Salām* and greeting to a Muslim then it is with the words, *Asalāmū ' Alaykum Wa Rahmatullāhī Wa Barakatuh.*

The Messenger of *Allāh* (ﷺ) spoke the truth when he said,

"He who is content with *Allāh* as his *Rabb*, with *Islām* as his religion and with Muḥammad (ﷺ) as His Messenger, has tasted the sweetness of *Īmān*."
(Reported by Muslim)[3]

Perhaps the reader will obtain some insights and beneficial lessons from this story in order to know and distinguish between the truth from the falsehood.

I ask *Allāh* that He benefits the Muslims through it and make it sincerely to seek His Noble Face.

Muḥammad b. Jamīl Zeno
1/1/1415 *Hijrī*

[3] [TN] *Ṣaḥīḥ Muslim Ḥadīth* no.34

BIRTH AND UPBRINGING

I was born in the city of Aleppo in Syria in the year 1925 AD[4] according to the passport which corresponds to 1344 *Ḥijrī* and currently I am approximately 70 years old. When I was approximately 10 years old I entered into a private school where I learnt to read and write. After this I joined the school known as *Dār al-Ḥufāḍh* and I remained there for 5 years, where I memorised the *Qur'ān* by heart with *Tajwīd.*

Then I entered a school in Aleppo which was known as the Preliminary Faculty of Sharī'ah which is now known as the *Sharī'ah* Secondary School and is a subsidiary to the Ministry of *Islāmic* Endowments. It is a school that teaches the sciences of the *Sharī'ah* and modern subjects. So I learnt *Tafsīr*, *Ḥanafī Fiqh*, Arabic Grammar, Morphology, History, the science of *Ḥadīth* and other subjects of the *Sharī'ah.* The modern subjects I learnt were Physics, Chemistry, Mathematics, the French language and other subjects which the Muslims from the past excelled in like Algebra.

I remember when I learned the subject of *Tawhīd* from a book called the *Ḥumaydī* Fortresses. It concentrated on *Tawhīd* of the *Rabb*[5] and proving that this Universe has a Creator and a *Rabb.* Only afterwards I realised that many of the Muslims, authors, universities and schools that teach the *Sharī'ah* subjects fall into this mistake. This is because the polytheists that fought the Messenger of *Allāh* (صلى الله عليه وسلم) used to acknowledge that *Allāh* is their Creator.

Allāh says,

"And if you asked them who created them, they would surely say 'Allāh' so how are they deluded?"

(Surah Zukhruf Āyah no.87)

---

[4] Regrettably the Gregorian calendar is widespread to the extent that it is also used in the Islamic countries except for Saudi Arabia. They rely upon the *Ḥijrī* calendar and it is mandatory because it is an Islamic calendar. It indicates the *Ḥijrah* in which Allāh gave Islām reverence.

[5] [TN] *Tawhīd Rubūbīyah*

Rather the *Shaytān*, may *Allāh* curse him, even acknowledged that his *Rabb* is *Allāh*.

Allāh the Most High said, while citing his statement,

"[Iblis] he said, My *Rabb*, because You have put me in error, I will surely make [disobedience] attractive to them on Earth."

(Surah Ḥijr Āyah no.39)

Therefore, as for *Tawhīd al-Ilāh*[6] which is the foundation whereby a Muslim attains salvation, then I didn't learn this and I didn't know anything about it. Thus, this is the situation for the rest of the schools and universities that don't teach it. Their students also don't know anything about it.

Whilst *Allāh* the Most High commanded all the Messengers (and Prophets) *('Alayhimusalām)* to call towards it [*Tawhīd Ulūhīyah*] and indeed the seal of the Prophets, Muḥammad (صلى الله عليه وسلم) called his people towards it. However they refused and became arrogant, just as *Allāh* informed about them,

"Indeed they, when it was said to them, "There is no deity worthy of worship in truth except *Allāh*," they became arrogant (and denied it)."

(Surah Ṣāfāt Āyah no.35)

As the Arab polytheists knew the meaning of it. They knew whoever said this would not be allowed to supplicate to anyone other than *Allāh*. Some Muslims say it [*Tawhīd Ulūhīyah*] with their tongues and at the same time call upon other than *Allāh*. Therefore they negate it [their own declaration of *Tawhīd Ulūhīyah*].

As for *Tawhīd as-Ṣifāt*[7], the school used to figuratively explain the *Āyat* of the *Ṣifāt* [of *Allāh*], regrettably just like schools in most of the Muslim countries and cities. I remember that a teacher used to explain *Allāh's* statement,

---

[6] [TN] *Tawhīd Ulūhīyah*

[7] [TN] *Tawhīd al-Asmā Was-Ṣifāt*

"The Most Merciful rose over (*Istiwā*) the Throne."

(Surah Ṭahā Āyah no.5)

Istiwā [rose over] to mean *Istawlā* [conquering, seizing, capturing] and then cited the following statement of a poet as proof,

Indeed Bishr (a commander) conquered 'Irāq without a sword and spilling blood

Ibn al-Jawzī said, it is not known who stated this poetry. Others have said he was a Christian.
The answer and explanation of the word *Istiwā* is in *Ṣahīh Bukhārī* when *Allāh* the Most High says,

"Then He rose over (Istiwā) to the heavens."

(Surah Baqarah Āyah no.29)

Mūjāhid and *Abūl 'Aāliyah* said, [the meaning of] *Istiwā* is to elevate and rise up. *Ṣahīh Bukhārī, Kitāb at-Tawhīd* vol.8, p.175

So is it allowed for a Muslim to leave the saying of the *Tabi'īn* in *Ṣaḥīḥ Bukhārī* and take the saying of an unknown poet?

This corrupt interpretation which rejects *Allāh* being elevated above His Throne is against the belief of *Imām* Abū Ḥanīfah, *Imām* Mālik and other than them. *Imām* Abu Ḥanīfah, the one whose *Maḍhab* they study and teach, said,

"Whoever says that I don't know if my *Rabb* is above the heavens or on the Earth, then he has indeed committed disbelief, because *Allāh* says,

"The Most Merciful rose over (Istiwā) the Throne."

(Surah Ṭahā Āyah no.5)

and His Throne is above the seven Heavens."

See *The Explanation Of Aqīdah at-Ṭaḥawīyah* p.322

I obtained my school certificates in 1948 and I acquired my general secondary school certificates. I passed my entry examination for al-Azhar (University), however because of bad health I wasn't able to go there and entered the teaching institute in Aleppo. I started teaching as a teacher for around 29 years and then I left teaching.

After I resigned from teaching I went to *Makkah* for *'Umrāh* in the year 1399 *Hijrī* [1979]. I was introduced to Shaykh 'Abdul Āzīz b. 'Abdullāh b. Bāz. He got to know that my beliefs were *Salafī* so he appointed me as a teacher at the *[Masjid] Haram* in *Makkah* during the *Ḥajj*.

When the season of *Ḥajj* finished he sent me to Jordan as a caller to *Allāh*. So I went, and I stayed at a city called *Ramthā* in the *Masjid* of Salāhudīn. Then I was the *Imām*, preacher and a teacher of the *Qur'ān*. I used to visit the middle schools and provide guidance to the students towards the belief of *Tawhīd*, so it was well accepted by them.

I came to *Makkah* for *'Umrāh* [again] in the year 1400 *Hijrī* [1980] in the month of Ramadhān and stayed there until after *Ḥajj*. I met and got to know a student from the students of *Dār al-Ḥadīth Khayriyyah* at *Makkah*. He requested me to become a teacher amongst them because there was a need for teachers there, especially [for teaching] the knowledge of *Ḥadīth* terminologies. So I called the Director of *Dār al-Ḥadīth* and he showed willingness [in making me a teacher there]. He requested me to obtain a reference and decision from the eminent Shaykh 'Abdul Aziz b. Bāz. So he wrote to the Director requesting that I should become a teacher amongst them. Thereafter I entered the school and I taught the students *Tafsīr*, *Tawhīd*, the Noble *Qur'ān* and other lessons etc.

Then with the grace and help of *Allāh* I started issuing small, concise and simplified booklets which became accepted in every land around the world. Some books were translated into English, French, Bengali, Indonesian, Turkish, Urdu and other languages.

I named them *'A Series Of Islāmic Instructions'* which has reached to more than 20 booklets, and they have been printed in the 100s and 1000s. Most of them have been given out for free. The reader of the booklets can find the names and numbers of the (series mentioned) on the back cover of them.

I ask *Allāh* that He benefits the Muslims with it and make it sincerely for Him, seeking His face the Most High.

I USED TO BE A *NAQSHBANDĪ*

Since childhood I used to attend the lessons at the *Masājid* and the circles of *Ḍhikr*. Once a Shaykh from the *Naqshbandī* methodology saw me and he took me to a corner of the *Masjid*. He began to give and tell me about the chanting of the *Naqshbandī* methodology. However, due to my young age I was unable to maintain what he ordered me from the chants. Nevertheless, I used to sit in a corner when attending their gatherings with my relatives and I heard what they used to say from the poems, eulogies and songs. Whenever the name of their Shaykh was mentioned they would start screaming out loudly with an elevated voice. This chaotic sound would aggravate and annoy me at night and cause me fright as well as illness.

When I got older, one of my relatives started taking me to the neighborhood *Masjid* so that I could partake in what they call the *Khatam*. We used to sit in the form of a circle and one of the Shaykhs would distribute pebbles to us and say,

[Recite *Sūrah*] *Fatiḥa Sharīf* and [recite *Sūrah*] *Ikhlās Sharīf*.

So we used to recite *Sūrah Fatiḥa* and *Ikhlās*, *Istighfār* as well as [send] *Ṣalāh* upon the Prophet (صلى الله عليه وسلم) based on the number of pebbles and in accordance to the way they had conserved. [The words of the *Ṣalāh* which] I remember from them are,

O *Allāh* send *Salah* upon Muhammad (صلى الله عليه وسلم) in accordance to the amount of animals there are.

They would say this in a loud voice at the end of their *Ḍhikr* and after it the delegated Shaykh of the *Khatam* would say,

Ar-Rābitah Sharīf

Their purpose of saying this was that they should picture their Shaykh whilst in the state of their *Ḍhikr* because according to their claims the Shaykh connects them to *Allāh*.

So they used to hum, shout and become overwhelmed with

reverence to the extent that I saw one of them jumping over the heads of those present from a high place due to the intense state of his *Wajd*[8] as if he was a circus performer. I was shocked by this behavior and the shouting during the *Ḍhikr* of the Shaykh's method.

Once I entered the house of this relative of mine and I heard a *Nashīd* from the *Naqshbandī* group saying,

Show me, I swear by Allāh, show me to the Shaykh who can help, show me

The one who can cure the sick and heals the insane

I stood at the door of the house and did not go inside. I told the owner of the house, does your Shaykh cure the sick and heal the insane?

He said, yes.

I said to him, the Messenger Esa b. Maryam *('Alayhisalām)* was given the miracle by *Allāh* to bring the dead to life and cure the lepers and he *('Alayhisalām)* said 'by the permission of *Allāh*'.

He said, our Shaykh does so by the permission of *Allāh* [also]

I said to him, so why do you all not say by the permission of *Allāh*!? Knowing that the one who cures is *Allāh* alone. Just like *Ibrahīm ('Alayhisalām)* said,

"So when I become ill then only He (*Allāh*) is the one who exclusively cures me."

(Surah Shu'ara Āyah no.80)

8 [TN] *Wajd* which essentially means esoteric trance accompanied with strange body movements. Here the Shaykh has mentioned a specific form of worship the *Sūfīs* do. When they hear fabricated *Ḍhikr*, eulogies and poems they go into a state of madness and insanity. This is what they call *Wajd*, *Tawajid* and *Samā'*. Apart from ripping their clothes they also dance, jump up and down, and move in really strange movements. The ignorant people then say that at this moment they have been connected to a higher spiritual plain and they have a direct connection with the divine which is incorrect.

AN OVERVIEW OF THE *NAQSHBANDĪ* METHODOLOGY

1. This methodology is characterised by its secretive and hidden customs as it does not involve dancing or clapping compared to the other famous [*Sūfī*] methodologies.[9]

2. Doing group *Ḍhikrs*, distributing pebbles to everyone, the delegated individual of the Khatam commanding them to say such and such, they put pebbles inside a cup of water [to soak] then drinking from that water in order to seek healing with it. These are all from the innovations in the religion which were rejected by the great companion Abdullah b. Masʾūd *(Radī Allāhū ʾAnhu)* when he entered the *Masjid* and saw a group of people in the form of a circle with pebbles in their hands.

One of them would say, recite *Subhān Allāh* in such and such way, do it in such a way to the amount of pebbles that are in your hands.

So he rebuked them by saying, what am I seeing you all do?

They said, O Abu *ʾAbdirahmān* these are the pebbles with which we count the number of times that we have said *Allāhū Akbar*, *Lā Ilāha Illallāh* and *Subhān Allāh*.

Abdullah b. Masʾūd *(Radī Allāhū ʾAnhu)* replied, then count your sins as I guarantee that none of your good deeds will go to waste [if you do this instead]. O Ummah of Muhammad (صلى الله عليه وسلم) [look at] how fast you are going towards destruction. These are the companions of your Prophet (صلى الله عليه وسلم) who are still available [and present in a large number], and these are his (صلى الله عليه وسلم) clothes that have not worn out yet and his (صلى الله عليه وسلم) utensils are not broken yet. I swear by Him in whose hand is my soul, perhaps you are on a religion more guided than the religion of Muḥammad (صلى الله عليه وسلم) or you are opening up the doors of misguidance.

---

[9] [TN] Just as those who perform *Qawālī* do these things. However in the Indian subcontinent some of the *Naqshbandīs* dance, clap and do nearly everything the Prophet (صلى الله عليه وسلم) forbade. Perhaps the *Naqshbandīs* in Syria didn't do this and Shaykh Muhammad b. Jamīl Zeno didn't have knowledge of them doing it in the Indian subcontinent.

(*Hasan*, reported by *ad-Dārimī* and *at-Ṭabarānī*)[10]

This is a rationally sound issue that they are either more guided than the Messenger of *Allāh* (صلى الله عليه وسلم), because they were given the ability, strength and success to perform an action [of worship], and therefore knowledge did not reach the Messenger (صلى الله عليه وسلم) [about these actions] or they are all on misguidance.

The first presumption is certainly rejected because there is no one more virtuous than *Allāh's* Messenger (صلى الله عليه وسلم) so there is nothing remaining except the other presumption [which is that those people have fallen into misguidance].

3. *Ar-Rābitatu Sharīf*: What they mean by it is to imagine that the image of the Shaykh is in front of them during *Ḍhikr* and that he is looking at them and watching them. That is why [during their *Ḍhikr*] you will see them bewildered and shouting in strange, horrible and indistinct sounds.

The level of *Ihsān* that was relayed in the words of the Messenger of *Allāh* (صلى الله عليه وسلم) is this,

"*Al-Ihsān* implies that you worship *Allāh* as if you are seeing Him, and although you don't see Him, without a shadow of a doubt He is seeing you."

(Reported by Muslim)[11]

So in this *Ḥadīth* the Messenger (صلى الله عليه وسلم) is instructing us to worship *Allāh* as though we see Him and even though we don't see Him, He definitely sees us.[12]

This level of *Ihsān* is only for *Allāh* alone, whilst they have given

---

10 [TN] *Sunan ad-Dārimī Ḥadīth* no.211. *Silsilah* as-*Sahīhah Hadith* vol.5, p.11

11 [TN] *Ṣahīh Muslim Ḥadīth* no.8

12 [TN] Meaning to know that He is observing every single action you are doing and knows exactly how you are doing it with all the minute details. This allows us to completely focus on the worship since when a person does an action and is mentally aware and reminded of the fact that *Allāh* is present and assessing them then the individual will take extra care and effort to do it correctly and right first time. They will also ensure to act with full devoted determination in order to receive full acceptance and acknowledgement of the action.

this to their Shaykh. This is from the polytheism which *Allāh* has forbidden. *Allāh* says,

"Worship *Allāh* and do not associate any partners with Him in anything [i.e. in any type of worship]."

(Surah Nisā Āyah no.36)

So *Ḍhikr* is a type of worship only for *Allāh*. It is not allowed for us to associate anyone with Him [in worship] even if they are Angels and Messengers *('Alayhimusalām)*. The *Shuyūkh* are of a lower rank than them so it would be an even higher level of impermissibility to associate them [in worship with *Allāh*].

The reality is that imagining the Shaykh during *Ḍhikr* is also present in the *Shādhilī* methodology and in other *Sūfī* methodologies as will come later [and be described further on in this book].

4. The severe shouting which overwhelms them during when the Shaykh is mentioned or when they seek help [in those things that only *Allāh* can provide help with] from other than *Allāh*, like from the *Ahlul Bayt* or from one of *Allāh's* pious people is from the rejected actions. Rather this is from the polytheism which is prohibited. So shouting during the *Ḍhikr* of *Allāh* is wrong because it negates and contradicts the statement of *Allāh*,

"In reality the [true] believers are those whose hearts shake[13] when *Allāh* is mentioned."

(Surah Anfāl Āyah no.2)

Additionally in the statement of the Messenger of *Allāh* (صلى الله عليه وسلم),

"…O people, show mercy to yourselves [i.e. don't raise your voices] for indeed you are not calling upon One who is deaf or absent. Indeed, you are calling One who is All-Hearing, Near to you and is He is with you."[14]

---

[13] [TN] Their hearts come back to reality because they become aware of *Allāh's* punishment and reward.

[14] [TN] The scholars of *Ḥadīth* clearly understood this the correct way. An example

(Agreed upon)[15]

Shouting, showing reverence and crying during the recollection of the *Awlīyā* of *Allāh* is more reprehensible because this indicates the joyfulness of the polytheists which *Allāh* referred to about them where He says,

> **"And when *Allāh* is mentioned alone, the hearts of those who do not believe in the Hereafter shrink with hatred[16], but when someone else is mentioned [in the acts of worship] instead of Him [their hearts become open and] they immediately become happy."**

(Surah Zumar Āyah no.45)

5. Exaggeration of the Shaykh's methodology. They believe that he can cure the sick whilst *Allāh* has mentioned the saying of *Ibrahīm ('Alayhisalām)* in the Noble *Qur'ān*,

> **"And when I become ill then it is only He [*Allāh* the One and only] who cures me."**

(Surah Shu'ara Āyah no.80)

Additionally, the story of the believing [Muslim] boy who used to make *Dū'ā* for those who were ill so *Allāh* used to cure them. When the King's companion [advisor] said to him, If you cure me then I will give you this wealth

So the boy replied to him by saying, I do not cure anyone, *Allāh* is the only One who cures. If you believe in *Allāh* I will make *Dū'ā* for

---

is how *Imām an-Nawawī* has put this *Ḥadīth* under the chapter heading in *Ṣahīh Muslim* as Chapter: It Is Recommend To Lower One's Voice When Saying Remembrance (*Ḍhikr*), Except In The Cases Where It Is Commanded To Raise The Voice Such As The *Talbiyah* Etc. (in the book of The Book Pertaining to the Remembrance of *Allāh*, Supplication, Repentance and Seeking Forgiveness)

15 [TN] *Ṣahīh Bukhārī Ḥadīth* no.2992 and *Ṣahīh Muslim Ḥadīth* no.2704

16 [TN] And they become irritated when the *Tawhīd* of *Allāh* is mentioned i.e. they don't even want to hear it because their disbelief and arrogance prevents them.

you then He will cure you.

(The story is reported by Muslim in his *Ṣaḥīḥ*)[17]

6. The *Ḍhikr* according to them is made with singular wordings. [Such as repeating the word] '*Allāh*' 1000s of times as part of their invocations. Whilst this type of *Ḍhikr* with the word '*Allāh*' [on its own] is not reported from the Messenger of *Allāh* (صلى الله عليه وسلم) and neither from the companions *(Radī Allāhū 'Anhum)*, *Tabi'īn* or the *Mujtahid Imāms*. Rather it is from the innovations in the religion of the *Sūfīs* because [grammatically] the word "*Allāh*" is the subject [of a sentence] and [in this type of *Sūfī Ḍhikr*] there is no predicate [and description or explanation of the subject mentioned] coming after it hence making the sentence and speech deficient.

If someone called the name ''Umar' repeatedly then we will say to him, what do you want from 'Umar? So if he does not respond to us except by saying the name ''Umar', ''Umar' we will say he has lost his mind and is crazy since he doesn't know what he is saying.

The *Sūfīs* cite the following saying of *Allāh* the Most High as evidence to make the singular *Ḍhikr*,

"Say *Allāh*"

[A part of the āyah in the *Qur'ān Sūrah al-An'ām Āyah* no.91]

If they had read the speech before it [the full *Āyah*], they would have known [the context] that what is meant is 'say *Allāh* revealed the Book'. The text of the *Āyah* is,

> **"And they did not appraise *Allāh* with true appraisal when they said, *Allāh* did not send down anything [i.e. revelation, guidance, a book] to a human being. Say, Who sent down the book that Mūsā *('Alayhisalām)* came with as light and guidance for the people? Which you [Jews] make it into pages, disclosing [some of] it and concealing much. And you were taught that which you did not know,**

[17] [TN] *Ṣahīh Muslim Ḥadīth* no.7148

[neither] you nor your fathers. Say, *Allāh*…"

i.e. say *Allāh* revealed the book.

HOW I MOVED TO THE *SHĀDHILĪ* METHODOLOGY

I became acquainted with a Shaykh from the *Shādhilī* methodology who had a good appearance and was very well mannered. He visited me in my house and I visited him at his house. I liked the gentleness of his words, his dialogue, his humility and his generosity so I asked him to teach me some incantations of the *Shādhilī* methodology. So he told me about some specific type of incantations of it.[18] He had a hermitage where some young men used to stay in which they would make *Ḍhikr* after *Jum'ah Ṣalāh.*

Once I visited his house and I saw pictures of many Shaykhs of the *Shādhilī* methodology hanging on the wall, so I reminded him about the prohibition of hanging pictures and he gave no reply despite there being a clear ḥadīth [on this topic] and it was not hidden to him. It is his statement (صلى الله عليه وسلم),

"Indeed, the Angels do not enter a house that has a picture in it."

(Agreed Upon)[19]

"The Messenger of *Allāh* (صلى الله عليه وسلم) prohibited having images in the house and he prohibited the person making them."

(Narrated by *Tirmidḥī* and he said it is *Hasan Ṣahīh*)[20]

Then after about year, I desired to visit the Shaykh whilst I was on the way to perform *'Umrāh.* He invited me with my son and one of my friends to dinner. After finishing he said to me,

Would you like to hear some religious *Nashīds* from these youngsters?

---

[18] [TN] If you study and look into the *Shādhilī* methodology very closely then you will notice that they have a lot of different types of *Ḍhikr* which are fabricated. Most of the time they claim that the Prophet (صلى الله عليه وسلم) came in a dream and specially taught them a specific type of *Ḍhikr* with so many virtues and told them to hold steadfast to it. This is falsehood since the religion is complete, see *Sūrah Mā'idah Āyah no.3*

[19] [TN] *Ṣahīh Bukhārī Ḥadīth* no.3322 and *Ṣahīh Muslim Ḥadīth* no.2106

[20] [TN] *Sunan Tirmidḥī Ḥadīth* no.1749 and *Silsilah as-Sahīhah Ḥadīth* no.424

So I said, yes.

So he ordered the youngsters who were sitting beside him, that had beautiful beards on their faces, to sing *Nashīds*. They started to recite the *Nashīd* [and poem] with one voice. The summary of it was, Whoever worships *Allāh* by being hopeful for His Paradise or through fear of His Fire then he has worshipped an idol.

I said to them, *Allāh* mentioned in an *Āyah* of the *Qur'ān* whilst praising the Prophets *('Alayhimusalām)* saying,

"...Indeed, they used to hasten to do good deeds, and supplicate to Us in hope and fear, and they were to Us humbly submissive."

(Surah Anbiya Āyah no.90)

So the Shaykh said to me, this *Nashīd* which the youngsters were reciting is by 'Abdul Ghani *Nablūsī*!

So I said to the Shaykh, are the words of the Shaykh [*Nablūsī*] given precedence over the words of *Allāh*? Whilst it even contradicts it?

One of the reciters said, 'Alī *(Radī Allāhū 'Anhu)* said, whoever worships *Allāh* in hope for His Paradise, then his worship is the worship of traders.

I said to him, in which book did you find this statement of 'Alī *(Radī Allāhū 'Anhu)*? And is it authentic?

So he was silent.

So I said to him, is it reasonable for 'Alī *(Radī Allāhū 'Anhu)* to contradict the *Qur'ān*, while he is from the companions of the Prophet (صلى الله عليه وسلم) and given glad tidings of Paradise?

Then my friend turned to them and said, *Allāh* the Most High has mentioned the attributes of the believers and praised them [with the following words],

"Their sides forsake their beds, to supplicate their *Rabb* in fear and hope."

(Surah Sajdah Āyah no.16)

They were all not convinced so I left debating with them and I went to the *Masjid* in order to pray *Ṣalāh.*

So one of the youngsters followed me and said to me, we are with you and the truth is also with you however we are not able to speak and refute the Shaykh.

I said, why don't you all say the truth?

He said, [if we say the truth then] he will remove us out from the place of residence.

This is a general initiation *Sūfī* principle. The *Sūfī* Shaykh advises his students that they should not object to the Shaykh no matter how wrong he is. They tell them a famous statement,

A murid is never successful that says to his Shaykh, why?

[Thereby] ignoring the saying of the Messenger of *Allāh* (صلى الله عليه وسلم),

"All the children of Ādam commit sins, and the best of those who commit sins are the ones who repent."

(*Hasan* reported by *Aḥmad* and *at-Tirmidḥī*)[21]

[In addition to ignoring] *Imām Mālik's* saying,

"Everyone's statement is taken or rejected [after comparing it with the *Sunnah*] except for the Messenger of *Allāh* (صلى الله عليه وسلم)."[22]

---

21 [TN] *Ṣaḥīḥ ul-Jāmi' Ḥadīth* no.4515, *Sunan Ibn Mājah Ḥadīth* no.4251, *Musnad Aḥmad Ḥadīth* no.13049

22 [TN] Meaning if his saying is in accordance to the statements of the Prophet *(صلى الله عليه وسلم)* or doesn't go against his *(صلى الله عليه وسلم)* statements in matters relating to the religion, and understood as per the companions then it is ok otherwise it will be rejected. This statement is famously attributed to *Imām Mālik* however in actuality this statement was mentioned by the people of knowledge before him such as Ibn ' Abbās *(Radī Allāhū ' Anhu)* and *Mūjāhid.* See *Qirā'atu Khalf al-Imām* p.213 by *Imām Bukhārī, Ḥilyatul Awlīyā* vol.3, p.300 by *Imām Abū Nu'aym* and *al-Madkhal Īlā as-Sunan al-Kubrā* vol.1, p.107 by *Imām Bayhaqī* and other than them.

GATHERINGS ON SENDING *DURŪD* AND *ṢALĀH* UPON THE PROPHET (صلى الله عليه وسلم)

I went with some Shaykhs to a *Masjid* in order to attend this gathering. So we entered the *Ḍhikr* circle and the people were dancing. They were holding on to each other's hands, swaying, going up and down. They were saying *Allāh*...*Allāh*...Everyone from the circle would come out of it to the centre and would gesture with his hands towards those people present to encourage them to become lively in movement and swaying. [This continued] Till my turn came to come out [of the circle and participate in this] and the chairman of the circle signaled to me to exit [the circle to the middle] in order to increase and encourage them to become lively and dance. [However] One of the Shaykhs that were with me [made an excuse for me and] said, leave him [to stay in his place] since he is weak.

This was because he knew that I didn't like resembling these actions and he saw me standing still and motionless so the chairman left me alone and excused me from going out to the middle of the circle. I heard poetry from beautiful voices however they were not free from seeking help and assistance from other than *Allāh*!

I noticed that the women were sitting in high places and watching the men. One of them was a young woman that was dressed up, unveiled with her hair, legs, hands and neck exposed.

I detested that in my heart and I said to the chairman of the gathering at the end of the session, indeed there is a young woman above us who is uncovered. If you advised her, alongside with all the other women, to wear the *Ḥijāb* in the *Masjid* it would have been a good deed.

He replied to me saying, we don't advise the women and neither do we say anything to them at all.

I said to him, why?

He said to me, if we advise them then they will stop attending the [gatherings of] *Ḍhikr*!

I thought to myself, there is no might or power except by *Allāh*. What kind of *Ḍhikr* is this in which the women are uncovered and no one advises them? Would the Messenger (صلى الله عليه وسلم) be pleased with this while he is the one who said,

"Whosoever of you sees an evil, let him change it with his hand;

and if he is not able to do so, then [let him change it] with his tongue; and if he is not able to do so, then with his heart and that is the weakest of *Īmān*."
(Reported by Muslim)[23]

[23] [TN] *Ṣaḥīḥ Muslim Ḥadīth* no.49

THE *QĀDIRĪ* METHODOLOGY

One of the Shaykhs of this methodology invited me and my teacher, who taught me Arabic grammar and Tafsīr. So we went to his house. After eating dinner, those present stood up for *Ḍhikr*. They started jumping around and swaying whilst saying *Allāh…Allāh*. I was standing with them but did not move. Then I sat down on the seat until the first duration finished.

I saw the sweat dripping from them so they brought a towel in order to wipe the sweat off. Since it was nearly midnight I left them and went to my home. The next day I met one of the people who were in the gathering with them and he was a teacher alongside me.

I said to him, how long did you all stay in that condition [last night]?
He said to me, till 2 hours after midnight [2am], after that we went back to our homes to sleep!

I said to him, and the morning [*Fajr*] *Ṣalāh* what time did you all pray it?
He said to me, we did not pray it on time we missed it.

I thought to myself, *Mashallāh* for this [unusual] *Ḍhikr* that makes you miss praying *Fajr Ṣalāh*.

Then I remembered the words narrated by A'isha *(Radī Allāhū 'Anha)* that she mentioned the attributes of the Messenger of *Allāh* (صلى الله عليه وسلم) and said,

"He (صلى الله عليه وسلم) used to go to sleep during the 1st part of the night and stay awake during the latter part."

(Agreed upon)[24]

These *Sūfīs* do the complete opposite. They stay awake during the 1st part of the night by doing innovations in the religion and dancing. Then they sleep at the latter part of the night and consequently miss the *Fajr Ṣalāh*. *Allāh* the Most High says,

"So woe to those who pray, who are heedless of their *Ṣalāh*."

---

24 [TN] *Ṣahīh Bukhārī Ḥadīth* no.1146 and *Ṣahīh Muslim Ḥadīth* no.739

(Sūrah Ma'ūn Āyah no.4-5)

Meaning that they do not perform the daily *Ṣalāh* at their fixed times. He (صلى الله عليه وسلم) said,

"The 2 [optional *Ṣalāh*] of *Fajr* are better than the world and whatever it contains."

(Reported by *at-Tirmidhī* and Shaykh Albānī graded it *Ṣahīh* in *Ṣahīh ul-Jāmi'*)[25]

[25] [TN] *Sunan at-Tirmidhī Ḥadīth* no.416 and *Ṣahīh ul-Jāmi' Ḥadīth* no.3517

CLAPPING THE HANDS DURING *ḌHIKR*

I was in a *Masjid* and there was a *Ḍhikr* circle after the *Jum'ah Ṣalāh.* So I sat down looking at them. In order to intensify their esoteric trance and rhythm one of them started clapping with his hands. I indicated to him that this is *Ḥarām* and not permissible, however he did not stop clapping. When he finished I advised him but he did not accept it. I met him after a while to remind him that this clapping is the actions of the polytheists when *Allāh* said about them,

"And their *Ṣalāh* at the House [*Ka'bah*] was nothing except whistling and the clapping of hands."

(A*l-Maka'* [meaning] whistling, *at-Tasdiyah* [meaning] clapping)[26]

(Sūrah Anfāl Āyah no.35)

So he said to me, but so and so Shaykh has permitted it!

So I thought to myself, the following statement of *Allāh* applies to these people,

"They have taken their scholars and monks as Rabbis besides *Allāh*, and [also] the Messiah, the son of Mary."

(Sūrah Tawbah Āyah no.31)

When 'Ādī b. Hātim *(Radī Allāhū 'Anhu)* heard this *Āyah*, whilst he was a Christian and had not accepted *Islām* yet, he said O Messenger of *Allāh* (صلى الله عليه وسلم) we do not worship them. So he (صلى الله عليه وسلم) said to him,

"Did they not make *Ḥalāl* to you all what *Allāh* made *Ḥarām* so you all made it *Ḥalāl*? They made *Ḥarām* what *Allāh* made *Ḥalāl* so you all made it *Ḥarām*?"

He *(Radī Allāhū 'Anhu)* said, yes.

He (صلى الله عليه وسلم) said, "So that was worshiping them."

26 [TN] *Tafsīr at-Tabarī* vol.13, p.522

(*Hasan* reported by *at-Tirmidhī* and *al-Bayhaqī*)[27]
I attended another *Ḍhikr* at another *Masjid* where the vocalist was clapping during the *Ḍhikr.*

After he finished I said to him, your voice was beautiful but clapping the hands is *Ḥarām.*

So he said to me, the tune of singing is not complete except with clapping. A Shaykh that is greater than you saw me and did not condemn me![28]

It is noted by those who have attended their *Ḍhikr* that they deviate [by distorting and saying atheistic things] in respect to the names of *Allāh.* So they all say [ridiculous things like],

...*Allāh*...*Aah*...*Hiya*...*Huwa*...*Ya Huwa*...[29]

This alteration and distortion is *Ḥarām.* They will be held accountable for it on the Day of Judgment.

---

[27] [TN] *Sunan at-Tirmidhī Ḥadīth* no.3095. This *Ḥadīth* has many benefits such as: 1. The legitimacy of teaching those who don't know; 2. Worship is a comprehensive term that includes all words and deeds, inward and outward; 3. Obedience to a created being that involves disobedience to the Creator is a form of worship to = the created being; 4. One is required to ask the scholars about unknown or unclear rulings; 5. The Companions were keen on learning.

[28] [TN] In places like India and Pakistan people go to the extent of reciting *Islāmic* poetry with music. Some even recite the poetry in the same rhythm as a song and it leaves the listener not knowing whether it is a song or a poem. Sadly this now also occurs in the West where people recite Islamic poetry in the rhythm and tune of a western song, and *Allāh's* refuge is sought.

[29] [TN] As well as other such words which carry no meaning that they dance to.

SELF-HARM WITH SKEWERS [WITH AN IRON SKEWER]

There is a *Sūfī* hermitage near our house. I went there to find out about their [way of] *Ḍhikr.* After the *Īshā Ṣalāh* the vocalists came. They were all clean shaven and beardless. They all started to say the following words in unison:

Bring the cups of Rāḥ [alcohol]

And fill them to the top

They would keep on repeating the poem whilst swaying. Their leader would repeat it himself then all the others would repeat it after him like a band of singers and musicians!

They had no shame whatsoever in mentioning alcohol whilst sitting in the *Masjid* that was made for performing *Ṣalāh* and reciting the *Qur'ān*. The meaning of *Rāḥ* in this poem is alcohol which *Allāh* the Almighty has declared *Ḥarām* in His Book. The Messenger of *Allāh* (صلى الله عليه وسلم) has done the same as mentioned in his (صلى الله عليه وسلم) *Aḥadīth.*

Then they started beating the drums ardently. An older person from them moved to the front, took his shirt off and started shouting with a loud voice, O grandfather!

What is intended by saying this is to seek help from one of his dead ancestors from the sons of the *Rifa'i* methodology because they are famous for doing this action![30]

Then he took hold of an iron skewer and inserted it into his skin and side whilst shouting, O grandfather!

Then a person in army clothing who was beardless came along. He took a glass and started biting it with his teeth! So I thought to myself that if this soldier is truthful [in defending his country and people] then why does he not go to the Jews [in Israel] and fight against them instead of breaking a glass with his teeth.

---

30 [TN] It is very famously known among them that they believe by doing this action their so called 'blessed' ancestors will help their followers during difficulties. This is a form of ancestor worship and we seek *Allāh's* refuge in that as *Allāh's* aid alone should be sought in times of ease and difficulties.

That was at in the year 1967AD when the Jews occupied and invaded a lot of the Arab land [of Palestine] and the Arab armies were defeated and lost the war. This soldier was also amongst them [and whilst he could break glass with his teeth], he was unable to do anything. Additionally, he was clean shaven and beardless.

1. Some people think that these types of acts are *Karāmāh* [miracle acts]. They did not know that these actions can happen from devils that are gathered around them and help support their misguidance.

This is because they turned away from the remembrance of *Allāh* and associated partners with *Allāh* when they sought help from their ancestors. Consequently making them in accordance with His, the Most High, statement,

"And whoever is blinded from remembrance of the Most Merciful – We appoint for him a devil, and he is to him a companion. And indeed, the devils avert them from the way [of guidance] while they think that they are [rightly] guided"

(Ṣurāh Zukhruf Āyah no. 36-37)

Allāh the Most High, makes the *Shayātīn* subservient to them so that they become even more misguided on account of the statement of *Allāh* the Most High,

"Say, Whoever is in misguidance, let the Most Merciful extend for him an extension [in misguidance, wealth and time]…"

(Ṣuraḥ Maryam Āyah no.75)

2. There is nothing strange about the *Shayātīn* helping them and giving them the ability to do that. Sulaymān *('Alayhisalām)* asked from his subordinates to bring the throne of the Queen Bilqīs,

"A powerful one from among the Jinn said, I will bring it to you before you rise from your place, and indeed, I am for this [task] strong and trustworthy."

(Ṣuraḥ Namal Āyah no.39)

For those who have been to places like India, such as Ibn Baṭūṭa the traveller and others, then they saw the Magians do a lot more than this![31]

3. The reality of these situations is that there purpose is not for truly attempting to validate *Karāmāt* or establish someone as being a *Walī*[32], rather self-harm with skewers etc. is actually from the work of the devils who gather around singing and music which is one of the

---

[31] [TN] They would have surely seen these type of circus acts performed by the Hindū *Jogīs* [Acrobats], Snake Charmers and Shaman. Nowadays one can see = these types of things commonly and most people understand them as nothing but illusion artists or street performers. Ibn Baṭūṭa was a person who was not entirely truthful about his travels or he must have been confused on some occasions. This is noticeable in regards to the story where he claimed that he saw *Imām* Ibn Taymiyyah. This is a complete lie because of many reasons but one should suffice. Ibn Baṭūṭa said he entered Damascus on the 9th of *Ramadhān* in the year 726 *Hijrī*. Whilst *Imām* Ibn Taymiyyah was put in prison from the 6th of *Sha'bān* the year of 726 *Hijrī* until *Ḍhul Qa'dah* 728 *Hijrī* where he died and did not leave the prison except in a coffin and on a funeral bier! See *Ṭabaqāt ul-Ḥanābilāh* vol.2, p.405 and other reliable books of history such as Ibn Kaṭhīr's *al-Bīdīyāh*, Ibn 'Abdul Ḥādī's biography of *Imām* Ibn Taymiyyah called *Al-'Uqūd ud-Durīyāh* p.259 & p.284. *Imām* Ibn Taymiyyah was put in prison 1 month prior to Ibn Baṭūṭa entering Damascus so how could he have seen him? Was the *Mimbar* of the *Jāmīyāh Masjid* of Damascus transferred into the prison cell!? Of course not!

[32] [TN] A *Walī* of *Allāh* is the pious believer who follows *Allāh's* legislation. *Wilāyah*, from which *Walī* is derived, implies a notion of closeness, whereas enmity implies a notion of remoteness. So, the allies of *Allāh* are those who perform deeds that bring them closer to *Allāh*. On the other hand, however, the enemies of *Allāh* are those whom He keeps far from Him on account of their evil acts that necessitate their expulsion and driving them away from Him. *Allāh*, the Almighty, classifies His allies under 2 categories, 1. Those who draw close to Him by performing the obligations, which includes performing all duties and avoiding all prohibitions. 2. Those who draw near to *Allāh* not only by performing what is obligatory, but also by doing supererogatory acts. When a slave observes these supererogatory acts constantly, this will eventually lead him to be loved by *Allāh*.

musical instruments and enchantments of the devils.

Most of those who do these actions commit sins. Rather they openly commit polytheism with *Allāh.*

So how can they be from the *Awlīyā* of *Allāh* and the people of *Karāmāt*? *Allāh* the Most High says,

"Unquestionably, [for] the allies of *Allāh* there will be no fear concerning them, nor will they grieve. Those who believed and were fearing [having *Taqwā* of] *Allāh*."

(Ṣuraḥ Yūnus Āyah no.62-63)

So the *Walī* is the believer who has *Taqwā* of *Allāh* and stays away from polytheism and sins. He seeks aid from *Allāh* alone during hardship and ease. A miracle may come to him naturally without seeking it and fame in front of the people.

4. Shaykh ul-Islām *Imām* Ibn Taymiyyah mentioned about the actions [so called miracles (!)] of these types of people [so called *Walīs* (!)], that these actions [of so called miracles] do not happen for them when they are reciting the *Qur'ān* or performing *Ṣalāh* because these are *Shar'īāh* compliant [acts of] worship which are from *Īmān* and are Muhammadan [from the *Sunnah*] which expels the *Shayāṭīn* to run away. Those actions are innovated acts of worship in the religion that are polytheistic, satanic, philosophical that attracts the *Shayāṭīn.*

5. The strange thing is that 1 person who was from those that were influenced by *Ṣufī'ism* [by the name Sa'īd Ḥāwī], was deceived by these falsehoods. He wrote about it and called towards studying the *Rifa'ī* methodology.

He recounts of an incident he heard about and said of it, "A Christian man told me that a person stabbed him [with a spear] in his stomach and so the spear came out from his back [painlessly, without any sort of harm occurring to him]…!!"

Then he said, "The person of this *Karāmāt* [miracle] may be an evil individual, so it is [the miracle] of his grandfather."

(Refer to the book *'Tarbīyatunā ar-Rūhīyāh* [*'Our Spiritual Upbringing'*] p.74)

So the writer takes the incident from a Christian man, and he may be a liar. So do *Karāmāt* occur for [and through] evil people? Also, when has it become hereditary?

The [fact is that] *Karāmāt* are for the *Awlīyā* and the people of *Taqwā*, it is not hereditary and nor is it [occurring] for an evil person.

If something supernatural occurs [which goes against the natural Universal laws and circumstances that *Allāh* has put in place] for an evil person then this is not called a *Karāmāt*, as Sa'īd Ḥāwī claimed.

Rather it is just a lure and enticement [by *Shaytān*] for them which increases them in misguidance. I have already mentioned previously that the Magians do things more severe than stabbing with spears![33]

6. Then a *Salafī* man commissioned one of those charlatans, who was stabbing himself with spears, to put a pin in his eyes. So he refused and became scared. This indicates that he enters a special type of spear into his flesh. Those who used to engage in such actions and then repented from it explained how [illusions occur from] the blood that flows from them [which is fake] and they wash it afterwards.[34]

7. An honest Muslim told me that he saw a soldier striking himself with an iron skewer of a specific type and he saw blood flowing from the place of the skewer (where he was stabbing his body). So when

---

33 [TN] The Magicians and *Hindūs* perform even greater illusions than skewering and piercing their bodies with knives which seem amazing to the onlooker. Just like how an illusion artist gets a person or a child, puts them in a box then covers them in a cloth whilst proceeds to slowly cut their body in half and separates each half moving them very far from each other. It appears as though the body has been = separated in two parts with the person still being alive. Whilst in the middle it appears as though there is a fountain of blood gushing out. Sometimes they create the illusion of the person's head being separated from the body and blood is flowing out from the neck but they are still alive. They do all these tricks under the cloth and behind the curtain, so would you call this *Karāmāt*? The sincere seeker of truth would not be deceived by or accept these parlour tricks as *Karāmāt*.

34 [TN] It is very easy to realise that items like knives which are used to hit the body are only those such as props used in acting scenes. Tricksters cunningly press the fake blood against their body in order to make it appear that it has come out of their body.

he was taken to his military commander he said to him,

"We will hit you on the legs with a rifle so if you are truthful (of being able to do *Karāmāt*) then be patient and bear it."

So when the beating was carried out the soldier started crying, shouting, howling and begging for help. He was not able to take the hitting and the soldiers began laughing at him and mocking him.

SUMMARY

The Messenger of *Allāh* (صلى الله عليه وسلم) did not strike [himself] with skewers nor did his companions *(Radī Allāhū 'Anhum)* or the *Tābī'ūn* and neither the *Mujtahid Imāms*. If there was any good in [doing] it they [surely] would have preceded us in [doing] it. However, it is from the actions of the innovators who came later on that sought help from the *Shayātīn*. The ones who [are polytheists] associate partners with the *Rabb* of the worlds.

The Messenger of *Allāh* (صلى الله عليه وسلم) warned us from these innovations, and he said,

"Beware of the newly invented matters, because every newly invented matter is an innovation [in the religion], and every innovation [in the religion] is misguidance and every misguidance is in the Fire."

(*Ṣahīh*, reported by *an-Nasā'ī*)[35]

The actions of these innovators is rejected due to his (صلى الله عليه وسلم) statement,

"Whosoever does an action that is not in accordance with what we are upon will be rejected."

(*Ṣahīh Muslim* [*Ḥadīth*] no.1718)

These innovators ask for help from the dead people and the *Shayātīn*, and this is from the polytheism which *Allāh* has warned us against due to His statement,

"Indeed, he who associates others with *Allāh* [in worship] – *Allāh* has forbidden him Paradise, and his refuge is the Fire. And there are not for the wrongdoers any helpers."

(*Ṣurah al-Mā'idah Āyah* no.72)

35 [TN] *Sunan an-Nasā'ī Ḥadīth* no.1578, *Ṣahīh ul-Jāmi' Ḥadīth* no.1353 and no.2549

The Messenger of *Allāh* (صلى الله عليه وسلم) said,

"Whoever dies while still invoking anything other than *Allāh* as a rival (*Nidd*) to *Allāh*, will enter the fire."

(*Ṣahīh Bukhārī*, [*Ḥadīth*] no.4497)

([The meaning of] *Nidd* [in the *Ḥadīth*] is alongside, comparison and/or a partner)

Every person who has this type of belief as them or helps them, then he will also be amongst them.

THE *MAWLAWĪYAḤ* METHODOLOGY

In our city there was a special settlement which was called the "*Mawlawīyaḥ* settlement". It was at a very big *Masjid* where the daily prayers were performed. In this settlement there were a lot of graves which had fences around them. There were also highly decorated stones built over all the graves which had *Qur'ānic Āyāt* engraved on it. There was also the name of each person in the grave and some poetry written on it. The *Mawlawīyaḥ* group used to establish a *Hadrah* [a type of *Ḍhikr* gathering] every Friday or on special occasions.

These people wore a *Kalakh* [which is a] long fez [hat] on their heads made of grey [coloured] wool. They would play the flute and some [other] musical instruments during *Ḍhikr* [gatherings] which would be heard from far away.

I saw an individual from them who was standing in the centre of their circle and was spinning around repeatedly and did not move from his position. Whenever these people used to ask for help from their Shaykh Jalaludīn Rūmī and other than him, they would bow their heads.

1. The strange thing is that the *Masājid* in many of the Muslim countries, including this *Masjid*, have dead people buried in them which is an imitation of the Jews and Christians. Whereas the Prophet (صلى الله عليه وسلم) said,

"May *Allāh's* curse be on the Jews and the Christians, as they took the graves of their Prophets as *Masājid*."

['Ā'īsha and 'Abdullāh b. 'Abbās *(Radī Allāhū 'Anhuma)* stated] He (صلى الله عليه وسلم) intended to warn [the Muslims] of what they [the previous nations Jews and Christians] had done.

(Reported by *Bukhārī*)[36]

Additionally, praying towards the graves is forbidden because the Prophet (صلى الله عليه وسلم) said,

"Do not sit on the graves and do not pray facing towards them."

---

36 [TN] *Ṣahīh Bukhārī Ḥadīth* no.4443, no.4444

(Reported by *Muslim* and *Aḥmad*)[37]

As for building on graves such as tombstones, domes, walls, writing on them and painting them, then listen to the prohibition of the Messenger of *Allāh* (ﷺ) about that. The companion Jabir *(Radī Allāhū 'Anhu)* narrated that,

"He (ﷺ) forbade plastering graves and building on them."

(Reported by *Muslim*)[38]

In another narration it is stated,

"He (ﷺ) forbade writing something on graves."

(Reported by *at-Tirmidḥī*. [Also reported by] *al-Hākim* and *adh-Dhahabī* agreed with him [on the grading of the *Ḥadīth* to be *Ṣahīh*])[39]

([The meaning of] *Yujsasu* [in the *Ḥadīth*] is plastering and painting)

2. As for the usage of musical instruments in the *Masājid* and during *Ḍhikr*, then this is a religious innovation which the latter day *Sūfīs* invented. Indeed the Prophet (ﷺ) declared music as *Harām* with his (ﷺ) statement,

"There will surely be people from among my nation who will consider illegal sexual intercourse, the wearing of silk, the drinking of alcoholic drinks and the use of musical instruments, as *Ḥalāl*..."

(Reported by *Bukhārī* in *Mu'alaq* [suspended] form. Also reported by *Abū Dāwūd* and declared *Ṣaḥīḥ* by Shaykh Albānī and other than him)[40]

It should be noted that the exception on musical instruments is the *Duff* on the day of *'Eīd* and *Nikāh* for the women.

---

[37] [TN] *Ṣahīh Muslim Ḥadīth* no.972

[38] [TN] *Ṣahīh Muslim Ḥadīth* no.970

[39] [TN] *Sunan Ibn Mājah* no.1563 and *Ṣahīh ul-Jāmi' Ḥadīth* no.6843

[40] [TN] *Ṣahīh Bukhārī Ḥadīth* no.5590

3. They used to move around the [different] *Masājid* to establish what is called [*An-Nubah*] which is *Ḍhikr* with musical instruments. They would stay up at night and the people of the neighbourhood would hear the reprehensible sounds of the musical instruments![41]

4. I used to know one of them who made his son wear the same [top hat] which the non-believers wear. So I took it discreetly and tore it apart but this *Sūfi* person became displeased by the tearing of the top hat and he censored me in anger. I said to him, I was overcome by protective jealousy for your son who wears the clothing of the non-believers. I also apologised to him.

This *Sūfi* used to hang a plaque in his office on which was written,

(O our great protector Jalaludīn)

I said to him, how do you call upon this Shaykh who cannot hear and neither respond?

So he remained silent.

(This was a summary of the *Mawlawīyaḥ* Methodology)

[41] [TN] In places like Pakistan the kettledrum is used in the villages to announce the *Ṣalāh* time or during *Ramadhān* at *Suhūr* time but has recently been replaced by the sound of a siren. This is not from *Islām.*

A STRANGE LECTURE BY A *SŪFĪ* SHAYKH

Once I went to one of the *Masājid* to listen to a lecture with a Shaykh. A number of teachers and Shuyūkh gathered for it. They were reading from a book called *'Al-Hikam'* [The Book Of Wisdoms] by Ibn Ajība. The lecture was in regards to the *Sūfī* way of achieving purification of the soul and one of them began reading a story from this book.

A *Sūfī* man entered a *Ḥamām* to take a bath. When he came out of the *Ḥamām*, he stole a towel that the owner of the *Ḥamām* gives to those who bathe. He allowed the end part of it to be uncovered and visible so when people would see it they would rebuke and scold him in order to humiliate and train himself according to the *Sūfī* way. So that is exactly what happened.

When he left the *Ḥamām* the owner of the *Ḥamām* caught up with him and he saw the edge of the towel under his clothes. So he rebuked him and said bad things to him whilst the people were listening to it and saw this *Sūfī* Shaykh who stole the towel from the *Ḥamām*. Indeed the people attacked him with insults and slander and say other things about him just like how people treat a thief. They took a bad image of this *Sūfī* man!!

Another *Sūfī* man wanted to train and humiliate his soul. So he carried a sack around his neck and filled it with walnuts then went to the market. Whenever he passed by a child he said to him, spit on my face so I can I will give you a walnut. [A fruit which children like].

So the child would spit on the Shaykh's face and he would give them a walnut. This is how the spittle of the street children, who were eager to take the walnut, appeared on the Shaykh's face and the *Sūfī* Shaykh was pleased.[42]

---

[42] [TN]This group of *Sūfīs* is well known as the *Malāmatīya* i.e. the self-humiliating blameworthy ones. They carry out acts of self-humiliation and blameworthy activities on purpose and consider by doing so helps make them closer to *Allāh* by lowering their ego. They believe that the more they humiliate themselves the closer and high in rank they will be with *Allāh* therefore becoming a *Walī* in this life and in the hereafter. The result of this belief system is that you will see them doing strange things. It is said that this group originated from *Nishapur*, an old town from *Khorasān*, in the 9th century see *Tarīkh Nishapur*. Unfortunately stories of the misguided group *Malāmatīya* are still present in the modern books of Indo-Pak *Sūfīs*,

When I heard these two stories I almost erupted with rage and my heart got upset about these corrupt (and over dramatic type of) teachings which *Islām* renounces.

Islām gave honour and nobility to humans as per *Allāh* the Most High statement:

"Indeed, We have dignified the children of Ādam, carried them on land and sea…"

(Surah Isrā Āyah no.70)

After we came out, I said to the Shaykh who was with me, [Is] this the *Sūfī* way of training the soul! Does it's training include acts of theft that are *Ḥarām* for which the *Sharī'ah* ruling is to cut off the hand of the thief? Or is it for you to be humiliated and the young commit the worst deeds? The religion of *Islām* rejects and rebukes these type of acts. Sound intellect, which *Allāh* has made as a sign of honour and respect for humans, also rejects them. Are these [words of] wisdom which the Shaykh named in his book *'Al-Hikam'* [The Book Of Wisdoms] by Ibn Ajība!!

It is worth noting that the Shaykh who is conducting the lectures has many students and followers. Once, the Shaykh announced that he wanted to perform *Ḥajj*. So his students enlisted with him and registered their names to accompany him on *Ḥajj*. Even the women started to enlist and they may have needed had to sell their jewellery for it. Eventually the number of people who wanted to go reached

---

such as the story of a *Sūfī* elder who wanted to carry out a blameworthy act in the *Masjid* to purify and train his soul so he stole somebody's piece of clothing in front of everyone until people caught him and gave him the nickname of 'The *Masājid* Thief' see *Fayzān Sunnat* p.306. Some of the *Sūfī* Shuyūkh also pay people to humiliate and swear at them openly in front of others in order to relieve their = anger see *Ihyā Ulūm ad-Dīn* vol.3, p.60. In this way the *Sūfī* Shuyūkh fame rises amongst the ignorant people. In order to lower their anger, ego and arrogance they prescribe themselves to carry out begging. They justify this by stating that the honour and dignity of oneself cannot be broken without humiliating it and there is nothing more humiliating and degrading than begging. Why do *Sūfīs* do such acts to humiliate themselves? This is because they consider it rewarding to do so. They fabricate statements such as making self-humiliation equivalent to worshipping *Allāh* for such and such amount of years. All of this is not from the true teachings of *Islām*. May *Allāh* guide them, *Āmīn*.

quite high and he collected a lot of money. Then he announced that he could not perform *Ḥajj* and did not return the money back to the owners, rather he devoured the money by *Harām* means. *Allāh's* statement became true on him:

"O believers! Indeed, many Rabbis and Monks consume people's wealth wrongfully and hinder ˹others˺ from the Way of *Allāh*..."

(Surah at-Tawbah, Āyah no.34)

I heard one of this followers, who was from the rich people that was active for the Shaykh, say about the Shaykh that he is the biggest charlatan and biggest fraudster!!

ḌHIKR IN THE *MASAJID* OF THE *SŪFĪS*

1. Once I attended a *Sūfī Ḍhikr* at a *Masjid* which was located in the neighbourhood where I lived. A man with a good voice came there in order to sing *Nashīds* and poems for them during the *Ḍhikr* at the circle where the people of the neighbourhood gathered. So among the poems which I remember hearing from this *Sūfī* was,

O people who know the unseen, help us, save us from harm, give us victory.

As well as various other expressions of seeking help and asking for help from those who are dead who cannot hear. Even if they could hear they cannot reply to them. They cannot benefit themselves let alone others.[43]
The *Qur'ān* referred to these type of people and He said,

"[O People] those who you invoke [for help] besides Him do not possess even the skin of a date stone. If you call upon them, they cannot hear your calls. And if they were to hear, they could not respond to you

---

[43] [TN] During the Pre-Islamic era it is known that there were 360 idols present at the *Ka'bah* which represented pious people of the past i.e. dead *Awlīyā*. So they used to be called upon in times of grief or hardship. The Prophet (صلى الله عليه وسلم) destroyed these idols and purified the *Ka'bah* from them so that people would call upon *Allāh* alone for help instead of these idols. Sadly in the Indo-Pak countries there are individuals who people call scholars and these so called scholars (!) still call upon the dead and idols. How strange is this! In fact one of them was Hājī Imdādullāh Makī. Once when he was present at *Makkah* he called upon these 360 idols when he had a hardship. You can hear this from his own mouth, "Once I was in a difficulty and it was not being solved so I stood in the *Hatīm* [which is considered being inside the *Ka'bah* the house of *Allāh*] and said, you people live here with 360 or more pious people present and you cannot even alleviate a difficulty for a poor weak person, so what type of illness do you cure? After I said this I started to perform supererogatory *Ṣalāh*. As soon as I started it a black person came and stood next to me and also performed *Ṣalāh*. My difficulty went away when he came. When I finished my *Ṣalāh* he also finished his and then went away." See *Karamāt Imdādīyah* p.57.

[and your *Dū'ās]*. On the Day of Judgment they will disown your worship of them. And no one can inform you [O Prophet] like the All-Knowledgeable."

(Sūrah Fātir Āyah no.13, no.14)

After leaving the *Ḍhikr* and it ending I said to the Shaykh, who was the *Imām* of the *Masjid*, that also participated in the *Ḍhikr*, this *Ḍhikr* does not deserve to be called *Ḍhikr* because I did not hear *Allāh* mentioned in the *Ḍhikr*, there was no supplication to *Allāh* and there was no request [of help] from *Allāh*. Rather I only heard calling upon men of the unseen. Who are the men of the unseen that have the ability to grant us victory, save us and help us.

So the Shaykh was silent. The greatest refutation of them is the statement of the Most High [*Allāh*],

"But those [false deities] you call besides Him can neither help you nor even themselves."

(Surah Ā'rāf Āyah no.197)

2. Another time, I went to another *Masjid* that had a larger number of worshippers and in the *Masjid* the Shaykh was a Sūfī who had followers. After the *Ṣalāh*, they stood up to do *Ḍhikr* and started bouncing and dancing while shouting really loudly with the words,

Allāh…Aah…Hee…

The singer approached the Shaykh and began to dance in front of him and swaying as if he were a singer or dancer. He was flirting with his Shaykh and the Shaykh was looking at him smiling with acceptance. Sometimes I used to go visit this Shaykh with my Shaykh, who was also a *Sūfī*.

Once we went to visit him after he had returned from *Ḥajj*. We sat and listened to him so he started talking about his travel in a really big and comfortable American car when he travelled from *Makkah* to *Madinah*. So I thought to myself, what is the benefit of talking about these things? It would have been so much better if he mentioned the social, spiritual and other collective benefits of *Ḥajj*, in fulfilment of

Allāh's statement,

"So they may be present to obtain the benefits for themselves [from the religion such as prayer, pilgrimage and forgiveness as well as worldly benefits such as meeting Muslims from everywhere and trading for a limited period of time]..."

(Surah Ḥajj Āyah no.28)

HOW DO THE *SŪFĪS* BEHAVE WITH PEOPLE?

1. I bought a shop from one of the aforementioned *Sūfī* Shaykh's students on a condition that he must act as a guarantor if the tenant is late in paying the rent, so he agreed to that condition. After a while, the tenant stopped paying the rent. So I went back to the previous owner who I bought it from but he refused to pay anything based on the excuse that he had nothing [no money] to pay. After a few days this *Sūfī* went for *Ḥajj* with his Shaykh. I was surprised [by this] and realised that he was a liar.

I complained about my situation to some of the close students of the Shaykh in regards to what this man did by cheating me and sold me the shop whereby the tenant does not pay the rent and he [as the agreed guarantor] does nothing about. [One of them] said to me, what can we possibly do with him?

If he was [truly] fair, he would have summoned him and asked him to fulfil the rights of the people [in this case my rights in obtaining the rent money]. I went several times to the guarantor's house and to his textile factory. So one of the Shaykh's students, who used to sing *Nashīds* and dance in front of the Shaykh, saw me he realised that I was looking for his friend. So I asked him to show to his friend and mentioned to him about his friend's deed.

Instead of doing justice to me [by taking me to the guarantor or telling me of his whereabouts], he showered me with obscene and insulting words. So I left [looking for] him and thought to myself these are the manners of the *Sūfīs* which the Messenger (صلى الله عليه وسلم) warned us about by stating,

"Whoever has the following 4 [characteristics] will be a pure hypocrite and whoever has one of the following [4] characteristics will have one characteristic of hypocrisy unless and until he gives it up.

1. Whenever he is entrusted, he betrays.
2. Whenever he speaks, he tells a lie.
3. Whenever he makes a covenant, he proves treacherous.
4. Whenever he quarrels, he behaves in a very imprudent, evil and insulting manner."

(Agreed Upon by *Bukhārī* and *Muslim*)[44]

[44] [TN] *Ṣahīh Bukhārī Ḥadīth* no.34

HOW I WAS GUIDED TO *TAWHĪD*?

I was reading to the Shaykh from whom I studied the *Ḥadīth* of Ibn 'Abbās *(Radī Allāhū 'Anhu)*, and it was his (ﷺ) statement, "When you ask then ask *Allāh*, and when you seek help then seek help from *Allāh*."

(Reported by *at-Tirmidhī* and he said it is *Hasan Ṣahīh*)[45]

So I was astounded by the explanation by an-Nawawī when he said,

"Then if there is a need that an individual asks for and it is not normal for it to occur at the hands of *Allāh's* creation, such as asking for guidance and knowledge…healing the sick and getting well-being [then] the individual asks for such things only from his *Rabb*...As for asking the creation [for things that are not in their power to do] and relying on them [in this regard], then it is a reprehensible act."[46]

So I said to my Shaykh, this *Ḥadīth* and its explanation indicate [and are proofs] that it is not permissible to seek help from anyone other than *Allāh*.

He said to me, rather it is permissible!!

I said, what is your evidence?

So the Shaykh got angry and shouted stating, my aunt says, 'O Shaykh Sa'd' [and he is buried in a *Masjid* where she can seek help from him], so I said to her, O my aunt, does Shaykh Sa'd benefit you? She said, 'I call upon him, so he intercedes to *Allāh* and He heals me!!'

I said to him, you are a man of knowledge who spent your life reading books then you take your beliefs from your ignorant aunt!

He told me, you have *Wahhābī* thoughts. You go for *'Umrāh* and bring *Wahhābī* books!!!!

I knew nothing about *Wahhābism* except what I heard from the *Mashaykh*. They said about them, the *Wahhābīs* are opponents of the people and do not believe in the *Awlīyā* and their *Karāmāt*. They do not love the Messenger *(ﷺ)* and other false accusations!

---

[45] [TN] *Sunan at-Tirmidhī Ḥadīth* no.2516 and *Ṣahīh ul-Jāmi' Ḥadīth* no.7957

[46] [TN] *Sharh Matan al-Arba'in an-Nawawīyah* by *an-Nawawī* p.63

So I thought to myself, if the *Wahhābīs* believe in seeking help from *Allāh* alone, and that the healer is *Allāh* alone, then it is mandatory that I get to know them.

Thus, I enquired about their group and they said that these people have a place at which they meet on Thursday evenings to give lessons on *Tafsīr*, *Ḥadīth* and *Fiqh*. So I went to them with my children and some educated mature youngsters. We entered a large room and we sat waiting for the lesson.

After a while an elderly Shaykh entered upon us. He gave us *Salām* and shook hands with all of us, starting with his right hand. Then he sat on a seat, and no one stood up for him. So I thought to myself, this Shaykh is humble, it is not enforced to stand up [for him]. The Shaykh started the lesson by saying, all complete Praise belongs to *Allāh*, we praise Him, we seek His aid and we seek His forgiveness…[continuing] to the end of the sermon in which the Messenger (صلى الله عليه وسلم) used to open his sermons and lessons. Then he began speaking in [a pure accent of] the Arabic language, quoted *Ahadīth* and explained its authenticity alongside its narrators. He would send salutations upon the Prophet (صلى الله عليه وسلم) whenever his (صلى الله عليه وسلم) name was mentioned.

At the end, questions were written on pieces of paper and asked to him so he answered them with evidences from the *Qur'ān* and *Sunnah*. Some of the people present tried to argue with Shaykh but he did not answer. He said in his last lesson, all complete Praise belongs to *Allāh* that we are Muslims and *Salafīs*.

Salafīs [They are those who follow the righteous predecessors: the Messenger (صلى الله عليه وسلم) and his (صلى الله عليه وسلم) companions]

Some of the people say that we are *Wahhābīs*, so this is [abuse, an insult and] name-calling. Indeed *Allāh* has forbidden us from this with His statement,

"…do not defame one another, nor call each other by offensive nicknames…"

(Surah Hujurat, Āyah no.11)

In the past, they accused *Imām ash-Shafi'ī* of being a *Rafidī* so he refuted them by saying:

If being a Rafidī means love for the family of Muḥammad (صلى الله عليه وسلم)

Then let the Humans and Jinn bear witness that I am a Rafidi[47]

We respond to those who accuse us of *Wahhābism* with the words of one of the poets,

If the one who follows Aḥmad is a Wahhābī

Then I affirm that I am a Wahhābi[48]

When it was finished, we left with some of the mature youngsters and they were impressed by his knowledge and humility. I heard one of them say, this is the real Shaykh!!!

---

[47] [TN] *Manāqib al-Imām Shafi'ī* by al-Bayhaqī vol.2, p.71

[48] [TN] *Al-Hadiyatu us-Suniyatu Wat Tuhfatu ul-Wahabiyatu un-Najdiyah* p.110

THE MEANING OF *WAHHĀBĪ*

The enemies of *Tawhīd* called the monotheists the word [*Wahhābī*] in reference to Muhammad b. ʾAbdul Wahab. If they were truthful, they would have said [Muḥammadi] in reference to his name [Muhammad]. *Allāh* willed it to be [*Wahhāb*] in regards to [*Al-Wahhāb*], which is one of the names of *Allāh*. So while the *Sūfī* is associated with a group that wears wool, the *Wahhābīs* are associated with *Al-Wahhāb*. *Allāh* is the one who granted him *Tawhīd* and enabled him to call to Him by the grace of *Allāh*.

DEBATE WITH A *SŪFĪ* SHAYKH

1. When the Shaykh whom I was studying with learned that I had gone to the *Salafis* and listened to Shaykh Muḥammad Nasirudīn al-Albānī, he became very angry because he was afraid that I would leave him and turn away against him. After some time, one of the individuals who lived by the *Masjid* came to us to attend the lesson with us in the *Masjid* after *Maghrib*. The Shaykh began telling us that he heard from a *Sūfī* Shaykh in one of his lessons that, the wife of one of his students had difficulty by labour pains and childbirth so he invoked for help from a young Shaykh [and he meant himself]. So she gave birth and the hardship went away from her.

The Shaykh we are studying with said to the individual, what is wrong in this?

The individual said to him, this is polytheism.

So the Shaykh said to him, be quiet you do not know what polytheism is and you are [merely] a blacksmith. We Shuyūkh have knowledge and we know more than you.

Then the Shaykh got up to his room and he brought the book *Al-Aḍhkār* by *Imām* an-Nawawī. He began to read the story of Ibn ʾUmar *(Radī Allāhū ʾAnhu)* that when his leg was numb he said, 'O Muhammad!!'

[The Shaykh then said], so [tell me] did he commit polytheism?

The man said to the Shaykh, this is *Daʾīf* [weak i.e. not *Ṣahīh*].

The Shaykh shouted angrily, you do not know the *Ṣahīh* from the *Daʾīf*, [rather] we are scholars we know that.

Then he turned to me and he said to me, if this man appears [in the lessons] again, I will kill him!

We left the *Masjid* and the man requested me to send my son with him to bring the book [*Al-Aḍhkār*] with the verification of Shaykh ʾAbdulqādir al-Arna'ūt. So he brought it and gave it to me. Thus the story was declared *Daʾīf* by the verifier.

The next day my son gave the Shaykh the book and he found out that the story was not *Ṣahīh* [but] in view of that he did not admit his mistake. He said, this is from the virtuous actions in which *Daʾīf Aḥadīth* are taken [accepted]!!!

I say, this is not among the virtuous actions as the Shaykh claims.

Rather, it is from the beliefs in which it is not permissible to take the *Daʾīf Ḥadīth* whilst knowing that *Imām* Muslim and others hold the view that the weak *Ḥadīth* are not to be taken in regards to virtuous actions. Those of the later scholars hold the view that it is permissible to take *Daʾīf Ḥadīth* in regards to virtuous deeds under many conditions that are rarely met. Additionally, this is a story and not a *Ḥadīth*. It is not from the virtuous actions rather, it is one of the foundations of belief, as I mentioned above.

On the following day we came to the lesson. After the Shaykh completed the *Ṣalāh* he left the *Masjid* and did not sit down as usual to [deliver] the lesson.

2. The Shaykh tried to convince me that seeking help from someone other than *Allāh* is permissible, like *Tawassul.* So he began to give me some books, including a book:

Annihilating The Rumours On The Issue of Tawassul by Zāhid Al-Kawtharī.

So I read it and thus it permitted seeking help from other than *Allāh.* When it came to the *Ḥadīth*,

"When you ask then ask *Allāh*, and when you seek help then seek help from *Allāh*."[49]

Al-Kawtharī said about it, its chains are flimsy [i.e. *Daʾīf*]. So he did not take it.

Note that the *Ḥadīth* was mentioned by *Imām* an-Nawawī in his book, 40 *Ḥadīth* no.19. The *Ḥadīth* was reported by *Imām at-Tirmidhī* who graded it as *Hasan Ṣaḥīḥ*. An-Nawawī and other scholars agreed on this. So I was amazed at how Al-Kawtharī rejected the *Ḥadīth* because it contradicted his beliefs. So my dislike for him and his beliefs increased. My love for the *Salafīs* and their beliefs increased, the ones who forbid seeking help from other than *Allāh*, based on the previous *Ḥadīth* and the words of *Allāh* the Most High,

---

[49] [TN] *Sunan at-Tirmidhī Ḥadīth* no.2516 and *Ṣahīh ul-Jāmiʾ Ḥadīth* no.7957

"And do not invoke [worship] besides *Allāh* that which neither benefits you nor harms you, for if you did, then indeed you would be of the wrongdoers."

(Surah Yūnus Āyah no.106)

[Additionally] His (صلى الله عليه وسلم) statement,
"*Dū'ā* is worship..."

(Reported by *at-Tirmidhī* and he said it is *Hasan Ṣahīh*)[50]

3. When my Shaykh saw that I was not convinced by the books he gave me, he stopped associating with me and spread rumours about me [that he is a *Wahhābī* beware of him]. I thought to myself, they said about our leader Muḥammad (صلى الله عليه وسلم) that he (صلى الله عليه وسلم) is [a magician or insane] and they said about *Imām* ash-Shafi'ī that he is a *Rafidī*, so he refuted them saying,

If being a Rafidī means love for the family of Muḥammad (صلى الله عليه وسلم)

Then let the Humans and Jinn bear witness that I am a Rafidī[51]

They denounced one of the monotheists due to being a *Wahhābī* so he refuted them by saying.

If the one who follows Aḥmad is a Wahhābī

Then I affirm that I am a Wahhābī

I negate partners with Allāh

For I have no other Rabb except the Unique, Giver

There is no dome that can be hoped for [in giving help], nor an idol

Nor can a grave have the causative means [to do so][52]

---

[50] [TN] *Sunan at-Tirmidhī Ḥadīth* no.2969 and *Ṣahīh ul-Jāmi' Ḥadīth* no.3407

[51] [TN] *Manāqib al-Imām Shafi'ī* by al-Bayhaqī vol.2, p.71

I praise *Allāh* completely who guided me to *Tawhīd* and to the creed of the righteous predecessors. I began to call to *Tawhīd* and spread it among people, following the example of the leader of humankind. He (ﷺ) was the one who began his (ﷺ) call to *Tawhīd* in *Makkah* for 13 years with his companions, enduring harm and [they] were patient until *Tawhīd* spread and the state of *Tawhīd* was established by the grace of *Allāh*.

[52] [TN] *Al-Hadiyatu us-Suniyatu Wat Tuhfatu ul-Wahabiyatu un-Najdiyah* p.110

THE STANCE OF *SŪFĪ SHUYŪKH* ON *TAWHĪD*

1. I published a 4 page pamphlet entitled:

'There is no deity worthy of Worship in Truth except Allāh, Muḥammad is the Messenger of Allāh, You alone we worship and You alone we seek help from, If you ask, ask Allāh, and if you seek help, seek help from Allāh'

I explained its meaning and I cited the saying of an-Nawawī in explaining the *Ḥadīth*, in addition to the statements of other scholars who called towards *Tawhīd.* In case the Shuyūkh say about the pamphlet that it is *Wahhābī*, I mentioned the [following] words of Shaykh ʾAbdul Qādir Al-Jeylānī from his book *'Al-Fatḥ Ur-Rabbānī'* [The Divine Conquest].

[His words are] ask *Allāh* and do not ask others. Seek help from *Allāh* and do not seek help from anyone else.[53]

Woe be to you, with which face will you meet Him tomorrow whilst you are disputing with Him in this world turning away from him, approaching His creation and associating partners with Him. You lower yourself by presenting and seeking your needs from them and you rely on them on the important matters![54]

Remove the mediation [and intercessors] between you and *Allāh*, for your adherence [and reliance] with them is self-obsession [and self-worship]. There is no rulership [and dominion], no power [and King], no riches and no glory except for the Truth [*Allāh*] the Almighty.[55]

Be with the Truth [*Allāh*], without the [need for intercessors from the] creation.[56]

[Meaning be with the truth by making *Dūʾā* to Him without an intermediary [or intercessor] from His creation]

This is a summary of the 4 page small pamphlet. The Ministry of

---

[53] [TN] *Al-Fatḥ Ur-Rabbānī* p.198

[54] [TN] *Al-Fatḥ Ur-Rabbānī* p.150

[55] [TN] *Al-Fatḥ Ur-Rabbānī* p.151

[56] [TN] Mentioned by Ibn Taymiyyah in *Majmū ul-Fatāwā* vol.8, p.338 and Ibn ul-Qayyim in *Madārij as-Salikīn* vol.p.63

Information allowed it to be printed, and 30,000 thousand copies were printed. My son distributed a few copies of it and he heard one of the Shuyūkh say that, this is a *Wahhābī* pamphlet.

It reached a big Shaykh in the country and he disapproved of it.

He requested to meet me so I went to his house and this Shaykh had studied with me at the *al-Khusruwiyyah* school in Aleppo which is now a *Sharīʾah* Secondary school. When I rang the bell, a girl came out and I said to her, Muḥammad Zeno.

So she went inside then returned and she said to me, he will come to the school shortly so wait for him there.

So I sat at the barber's shop adjacent to his house until he came out. I caught up with him and said to him, what do you want from me?

He said to me, I do not want [you to distribute] this pamphlet.

So I said to him, why?

He said, we do not want it.

When we reached the school gate I said to him, I will enter the school with you and read the pamphlet.

He said, I don't have time [to listen to that]!

I told him, I printed 30,000 copies of it and it cost us money and effort, so what do we do with them, do we burn them?

He said to me, yes burn it!!

I thought to myself, I will go to Shaykh Muḥammad as-Salqini who was my teacher in *Ḥanafī* Fiqh. So I went to him and said to him, I have a small pamphlet and one of the Shuyūkh said to me to 'burn it'.

He said to me, read it to me.

So I read it to him.

He said to me, this pamphlet contains the *Qurʾān* which is the word of *Allāh* and it contains the *Aḥadīth* of the Messenger of *Allāh* (صلى الله عليه وسلم). How can we burn it?

I said to him, may *Allāh* reward you with good. I will distribute it and not burn it.

After a while I distributed it and I found that it was well received amongst the educated youth to the extent that I found someone who printed and distributed it in the *al-Watar* Library at *al-Miskiyah* in the city of Damascus.

So I praised *Allāh* for aiding someone to print and distribute this pamphlet for free so that it's benefit may spread. I remembered the statement of *Allāh* Almighty that,

"They want to extinguish the light of *Allāh* with their mouths, but *Allāh* refuses except to perfect His light, although the disbelievers dislike it. It is He who has sent His Messenger with guidance and the religion of truth to manifest it over all religion, although they who associate others with *Allāh* dislike it."

(Surah Tawbah Āyah no.32, no.33)

Then I published this pamphlet in my book *'Minhāj al-Firqah an-Nājiyah'* [The Methodology Of The Saved Sect]

So whoever wants to read it should read the aforementioned book and you will find it with the same chapter heading that were mentioned above.

2. One of the Shuyūkh gave me a book as a gift containing the famous story of Tha'labah. When he wanted to reprint the book, I advised him to refer to the sayings of the scholars.[57] In particular [statements] in the book *Al-Isābah Fi Asmā' As-Sahābah* by Ibn Ḥajar [because] he and others have pointed out that it was not *Ṣahīh*. [However] the Shaykh did not accept the advice and he said to me, you are enthusiastic, leave these issues!

I said, if it is left off then I will call to the *Tawhīd* which the Messenger (صلى الله عليه وسلم) taught to his cousin 'Abdullāh b. 'Abbās *(Radī Allāhū 'Anhu)* when he was a boy. The Messenger of *Allāh* (صلى الله عليه وسلم) said to him *(Radī Allāhū 'Anhu)*,

"O boy! I will teach you some words…When you ask then ask *Allāh*, and when you seek help then seek help from *Allāh*."

To the end of the *Ḥadīth* mentioned by an-Nawawī and *at-Tirmidḥī* said it is (*Hassan Ṣahīh*).[58]

He said to me, we ask other than *Allāh*!!!

And with complete unflinching rudeness and bad manners rejected the *Ḥadīth* and opposed the statement of *Allāh* the Most

---

[57] [TN] Since the evidence of this story is very weak and the incident is exaggerated.

[58] [TN] *Sunan at-Tirmidḥī Ḥadīth* no.2516 and *Ṣahīh ul-Jāmi' Ḥadīth* no.7957

High,

"And do not invoke [worship] besides *Allāh* that which neither benefits you nor harms you, for if you did, then indeed you would be of the wrongdoers [i.e. the polytheists]."

(Surah Yunus Āyah no.106)

Then a few years later this Shaykh, who asks from other than *Allāh*, [1 of] his sons was killed and 2 [others] were put in prison. He left his home and migrated to another country. No one could help him at this point. *Allāh* destined me to meet this Shaykh at the honourable *Masjid al-Harām* of *Makkah*. I hoped that he had come to his senses and has returned to *Allāh*, asking Him [alone] for forgiveness, protection and help. So I greeted him [with *Salām*] and I told him, *Inshā Allāh* we will return to our country and *Allāh* will relieve us. So it is upon us to turn to *Allāh* and ask Him [alone] for help and support since He alone is capable, [what] do you think?

He said to me, the issue contains a difference [of opinion].
I said to him, what is the difference [of opinion]? You are the *Imām* of a *Masjid* and you recite in your *Ṣalāh* in every *Rak'ah,*

"It is You alone that we worship and You alone that we ask for help."

(Surah Fatiḥa Āyah no.5)

The Muslim repeats it dozens of times in his day, especially in his *Ṣalāh.*

[However] this *Sūfī Naqshbandī* Shaykh did not withdraw from his mistake. Rather he insisted and began to argue that it is a matter in which there is a differing in order to justify his incorrect position!

The polytheists who were fought by the Messenger of *Allāh* (صلى الله عليه وسلم) used to call upon their *Awlīyā* in times of prosperity but when they fell into hardship or distress they would ask *Allāh* alone [for help] as *Allāh* the Most High said about them,

"It is He who enables you to travel on land and sea until, when you are in ships and they sail with them by a good wind and they rejoice therein, there comes a storm wind and the waves come upon them from every place and they expect to be engulfed, they supplicate *Allāh*, sincere to Him in religion, [saying] 'If You should save us from this, we will surely be among the thankful'."

(Surah Yunus Āyah no.22)

Additionally, He said about the polytheists,

"...Then when adversity touches you, to Him you cry for help."

(Surah Nahl Āyah no.53)

3. I once went to a great Shaykh who had students and disciples. He was a preacher and an *Imām* of a large *Masjid*. I began to talk with him about *Dūʾā* and that it is an act of worship in which it is not permissible except for *Allāh* alone.

I brought him evidence from the *Qurʾān* which is the statement of the Most High,

"Say, 'Invoke those you have claimed [as deities] besides Him, for they do not possess the [ability for] removal of adversity from you or [for its] transfer [to someone else]. Those whom they invoke [Such as Angels, Prophets, deceased scholars, etc.] seek means of access to their *Rabb*, [striving as to] which of them would be nearest, and they hope for His mercy and fear His punishment. Indeed, the punishment of your Lord is ever feared."

(Surah Isrā Āyah no.56, no. 57)

[So I said to him], what is meant by His statement **'Those whom they invoke'**?

He said to me, the Idols.
I said to him, the intended meaning is the *Awlīyā* and the righteous people...

He said to me, let us refer back to the *Tafsīr* of Ibn Kathīr.
So he searched his library and brought out *Tafsīr* Ibn Kathīr. He found the commentator quoting many statements [regarding the interpretation] among which the most correct and authentic of them is the narration of Al-Bukhārī which states,

"People from amongst the humans used to worship people from the Jinn. Those Jinn embraced *Islām* but those human beings stuck to their [old] religion [of worshipping the Jinn]."
(vol.3 p.46)[59]

The Shaykh said to me, you are right.
So I was happy with this confession that the Shaykh said and I began to visit him regularly and sit in his room. Once I was surprised with him [when] he said to those [people who were] present,

"The *Wahhābīs* are halfway disbelievers because they don't believe in the souls.

So I thought to myself, the Shaykh renounced [his view] and feared for his position, so he slandered the *Wahhābīs*. The *Wahhābīs* do not deny the belief [and existence] of the souls because it is established from the *Qur'ān* and the *Ḥadīth*. However, what they do deny is [the view] that the soul has the ability and disposition to influence and make changes [to people's affairs] such as relieving the distressed, helping the living, benefiting them and harming them.

Since this is from the major polytheism that the *Qur'ān* mentioned about in regards to the dead with *Allāh's* statement,

"...And those whom you invoke other than Him do not possess [as much as] the membrane of a date seed. If you invoke them, they do not hear your supplication; and if they heard, they would not respond to you. And on the Day of Resurrection they will deny your association [of partners in worship with *Allāh*]. And none can inform you like [one] Aware [of all matters]."

[59] [TN] *Ṣaḥīḥ Bukhārī Ḥadīth* no.4714

(Surah Fātir Āyah no.13, 14)

These *Āyāt* clearly state that the dead do not have ownership [and power] over anything. Additionally, they do not hear the supplication of others. Even if it was assumed that they can hear them they would not be able to answer. On the Day of Judgment they will reject this polytheism which is clearly stated in the *Āyah*,

> **"...And on the Day of Resurrection they will deny your association [of partners in worship with *Allāh*]."**

(Surah Fātir Āyah no.14)

NO ONE KNOWS THE UNSEEN EXCEPT FOR *ALLĀH*

I was with some of the Shuyūkh in the neighbourhood *Masjid* studying the *Qur'ān* after Fajr and they were all memorisers of the noble *Qur'ān*. Whilst reciting the *Qur'ān* we went passed the following [*Āyah*], where *Allāh* the Most High stated,

"Say, "None in the heavens and earth knows the unseen except *Allāh*, and they do not perceive when they will be resurrected."

(Surah Naml Āyah no.65)

So I said to them, indeed this *Āyah* is clear evidence that nobody knows the unseen except for *Allāh*.

So they stood up to me and said, the *Awlīyā* know the unseen!!

I said to them, what is your evidence?

Then each one of them began to tell a story that he heard from some people that so-and-so *Walī* informs about the unseen things![60] So I said to them, these stories may be false and they are not evidence, particularly because they contradict the *Qur'ān*. So how can you take them and leave the *Qur'ān*?!!

---

[60] [TN] Some *Sūfīs* have gone to the extreme extent of relating stories about animals, such as donkeys, demonstrating knowledge of the unseen and therefore making analogy that on this basis humankind are more worthy of having knowledge of the unseen. One of them related a story that a donkey from Egypt had knowledge of the unseen. The story is that, "…something belonging to a person was placed with another person and then the donkey was asked where it is. The donkey was blindfolded, so he went around the entire congregation and pointed out to the person who kept the belongings of another person." See *Malfūḍhat Aḥmad Raza* vol.4, p.10-11.
Others who are always trying to declare themselves as monotheists regrettably forget the statements of their elders and refuse to reject their incorrect beliefs. An example of this is when one of them said that, "…people say that the knowledge of the unseen does not belong to the Prophets and *Awlīyā*. I say that the people of truth, wherever they look, discover and understand the unseen." See *Shamā'im Imdādiyah Malfūḍhat Haji* p.185. However as clearly noted these false beliefs go against what is related in the *Qur'ān* and *Sunnah*.

However they were not convinced and some of them started shouting and getting angry. I did not find any of them who took the *Āyah* [from the *Qur'ān* as evidence]. Rather they all agreed on falsehood and their evidence was fairy tales which they passed on that have no basis.

I came out of the *Masjid* and did not attend with them on the next day. Rather, I sat with the children and recited the *Qur'ān* with them which is better for me than sitting with those who have memorised the *Qur'ān* and oppose its creed and do not apply its rulings. It is obligatory for a Muslim, if he sees such people not to sit with them, in obedience to the statement of the Most High,

"…And if *Shaytān* should cause you to forget, then do not remain after the reminder with the wrongdoing people."

(Surah An'ām Āyah no.68)

These are wrongdoers who have associated servants with *Allāh* who they claim know the unseen. *Allāh* addresses His Messenger (صلى الله عليه وسلم) and commands him (صلى الله عليه وسلم) to say to the people,

"Say, 'I hold not for myself [the power of] benefit or harm, except what *Allāh* has willed. And if I knew the unseen, I could have acquired much wealth, and no harm would have touched me. I am not except a warner and a bringer of good tidings to a people who believe.'"

(Surah 'Arāf Āyah no.188)

Those who have memorised the Book of *Allāh* [mentioned previously] then the *Qur'ān* will be a proof against them and not for them, as he (صلى الله عليه وسلم) said,

"…And the *Qur'ān* is a proof for you or against you."

(Reported by Muslim)[61]

---

[61] [TN] *Ṣaḥīḥ Muslim Ḥadīth* no.223

Allāh sets an example for those who do not act according to the books which have been revealed such as the Torah. He said,

"The example of those who were entrusted with the Torah and then did not take it on [by not putting its teachings into practice] is like that of a donkey who carries volumes [of books but does not benefit from their contents]. Wretched is the example of the people who deny the signs of *Allāh*. And *Allāh* does not guide the wrongdoing people."

(Surat Jum'ah Āyah no.5)

This *Āyah*, even though it is against the Jews who knew the Torah and did not act according to it, then [similarly] it applies to everyone who knows the *Qur'ān* and does not act according to it.

The Messenger (صلى الله عليه وسلم) sought refuge from knowledge which does not benefit and said,
"O *Allāh*, I seek refuge in You from knowledge that does not benefit."

(Reported by Muslim)[62]

[i.e. I do not act upon it, nor convey it to anyone else, nor the knowledge that does not change my bad conduct].

In [another] *Ḥadīth*,
"Read the *Qur'ān* and act upon it, and do not eat by it..."

(*Ṣahīh*, reported by Aḥmad and others)[63]

5. I used to pray at a *Masjid* that was near my house and the *Imām* of the *Masjid* knew me. He found out from me about calling towards *Tawhīd* and to not supplicate to anyone else. So he gave me a book

---

[62] [TN] *Ṣaḥīḥ Muslim Ḥadīth* no.2722
[63] [TN] *Musnad Aḥmad Ḥadīth* no.15529

called '*Al-Kafi Fī Rad Ala Al-Wahhābī*' (*That Which Is Sufficient In Refuting The Wahhābī*) and I think that it was authored by Zayni Dahlan who was a Mufti in *Makkah* before the Saudi rule. He says in it, indeed there are men who say to something 'be' and it is!

So I was shocked at this false statement because this is one of the attributes of *Allāh* alone and humankind are powerless to [even] create flies. Rather, they are unable to recover what the flies took from their food.

Allāh the Most High has set an example for people to explain and make evident the weakness of creatures, He said,

"O people, an example is presented, so listen to it. Indeed, those you invoke besides *Allāh* will never create [as much as] a fly, even if they gathered together for it [i.e., that purpose]. And if the fly should steal from them a [tiny] thing, they could not recover it from him. Weak are the pursuer and pursued."

(Surat Ḥajj Āyah no.73)[64]

So I took the book to its owner and he had memorized the *Qur'ān* with me at the *Dar ul-Huffadh*, so I said to him, this Shaykh claims that men say to something 'be' and it is. Is this correct?

He said to me, yes and this is what the Messenger of *Allāh* (صلى الله عليه وسلم) said 'Be Tha'labah' so it was Tha'labah!

I said to him, was Tha'labah non-existent, so the Messenger (صلى الله عليه وسلم) brought him into existence out of nowhere [?]. Or was he absent and he (صلى الله عليه وسلم) was waiting for him since he was late. So when the Messenger of *Allāh* (صلى الله عليه وسلم) saw a shadow from afar, he was optimistic and said 'Be Tha'labah' as if he (صلى الله عليه وسلم) was saying I pray to *Allāh* that the next one [coming] is Tha'labah so that the army marches and does not delay. So *Allāh* answered his (صلى الله عليه وسلم) *Dū'ā* and the next one [coming] was Tha'labah.

The man was silent and he realised the invalidity of the words of

---

64 [TN] A comparison is made here to the worshipper of a false deity and that which he worships.

the Shaykh who authored it. The book is still with its owner.

A TRIP WITH THE *TABLĪGHĪ JAM'ĀT*

1. The *Tablīghī Jam'āt*[65] has a wide activity in the Arab and *Islāmic* countries, even in foreign countries such as France and other countries. This group is distinguished [and well known] for humility in its travels, sincerity in their preaching, organisation in their travelling, food and going out [to preach]. Their location of work is done at the *Masājid* where they stay. They go to cafes and other places to bring the people from there to the *Masājid* in order to perform the *Ṣalāh*. One of its members delivers a speech to those gathered in the *Masjid* [usually after the *Ṣalāh*] and this is a good practice.

2. The group has a leader named Shaykh In'ām Al-Hassan whose permanent residence is in Pakistan. They have a general [annual] conference and gathering, often in Pakistan [at *Raiwand* City]. In every country they have a leader whose opinion they take when consulting.[66]

They have a book called (*Tablīghī Nisāb*)[67] in the Urdu language. It is translated into Arabic and the scholars have criticised it in terms of [its ideology surrounding] creed. It contains *Sūfī* ideas and other things.

The books which they rely on the most are:

---

[65] [TN] The *Tablīghī Jam'āt* is a group built on the foundations of *Sūfism* and monasticism, whose initial purpose was to inspire and persuade people towards the religion. However from the very beginning, ignorant and misguided notions of *Sūfism* were nurtured in its foundations. Although they recite the *Qur'ān* and read the *Aḥadīth* within their gatherings they also relate fabricated *Aḥadīth*, fairy tales, stories of so called *Awlīyā* and special thoughts which contain blatant polytheism. Sadly when challenged on the polytheistic stories they are never ready to leave them as they wholeheartedly trust everything their elders state blindly with no room for questioning. They consider it wrong to do research because according to them they are blind followers and research is forbidden for them. Thus their call is not a call to *Islām*, but they have become the spokesperson of a new modern *Sūfī* sect which continuously regurgitates polytheistic narrations.

[66] [TN] India is another country in which they hold an annual conference and this is where the *Tablīghī Jam'āt* was founded.

[67] [TN] Also referred to as *Faḍhāil 'Amāl*.

- *Riyādh us-Ṣalihīn* [*Gardens Of The Righteous*]. It is a good book, especially the edited version that shows the *Ṣahīh Aḥadīth* from the *Da'īf*, and this is very important amongst the people of knowledge.
- *Hayat us-Sahabah* [*The Life Of The Companions*]. It is a good book [however] it contains *Da'īf* and fabricated *Aḥadīth* which requires [further] investigation and source referencing as will be explained later *Inshā Allāh*.

They have six qualities that they adhere to and they teach them to the members of their group which will be discussed later. These [qualities and] their conditions are as follows:

1. Fulfilling the word [That there is no deity worthy of worship in truth except *Allāh* alone and that Muḥammad is the Messenger of *Allāh*]
2. Establishing *Ṣalāh* with reverence and humility
3. Knowledge with *Ḍhikr*
4. Honouring Muslims
5. Sincerity of intention to *Allāh* the Most High
6. Calling to *Allāh* the Most High

GOING OUT WITH THE *TABLĪGHĪ JAMʾĀT* FOR *DA'WAH*

I was initially impressed by their *Daʾwah* and I went out with them to different countries.

1. I went out with them in the city of Aleppo in which I live. We walked around to the different *Masājid* especially on Friday. So we went out as a group to a neighbourhood of Aleppo called (Qarlaq) which has a large *Masjid* and I entered the *Masjid* before the Friday *Ṣalāh.* I went out with my aunt's son [cousin brother], based on the instructions of the [Jamʾāt] leader, to the market. We entered a (large cafe) in which people were playing backgammon and cards. The cards had pictures of a child, a girl and an old man. Our mission was limited to calling people to *Ṣalāh.* So we invited them and they responded [positively by joining us for *Ṣalāh*], except for a few of them that promised to complete the game and then come to the *Masjid.*

When we finished touring the marketplaces we went to the *Masjid* and the leader was waiting for us. When we arrived, he gave me the book *Riyādh us-Ṣalihīn* and requested me to read from the [the chapter about] etiquettes of the *Masjid.* So I read in it what the Prophet (صلى الله عليه وسلم) said,

"Whoever has eaten garlic or onion should keep away from us and should keep away from our *Masjid* and sit in his house."

(Agreed Upon)[68]

I explained to those present in the *Masjid* about the *Ḥadīth* and I explained to them that the smell of smoke [from cigarettes] is worse than the smell of garlic and onions. So the Muslim should avoid it because it harms his body, harms his neighbour, destroys his wealth and there is no benefit in smoking…

Suddenly the leader was staring at the book I was reading, which was *Riyādh us-Ṣalihīn*, as if he was [drawing attention and] saying to me, this speech about smoking is not found in the book, so don't talk

[68] [TN] *Ṣaḥīḥ Bukhārī Ḥadīth* no.5452

about it!

This is incorrect because smoking is widespread among Muslims, to the extent [that] it [smoking] is [done] amongst those who [also] pray so it is necessary to warn against it especially when warning against eating garlic and onions when entering the *Masjid*.

I noticed that some *Da'īf Aḥadīth* [were circulated and propagated] among the people (*Tablīghī Jam'āt*), so I mentioned that to them and they said to me, come with us to the general leader who is in Jordan and talk to him about that.

2. I went with the group to the city Hama. We used to knock on the doors and the owner of the house would come out. The leader [from the group] would invite him to come to the *Masjid* to meet with them and hear the lesson and the lecture. I entered upon their leader in their *Masjid* and he said to the groups of people present, we prostrated to *Allāh* so *Allāh* made the world prostrate for us!!

This is an enormous error. Prostration is an act of worship that is not permissible for anyone other than *Allāh*. *Allāh* the Most High said,

"So prostrate to *Allāh* and worship [Him]."

(Surah Najm Āyah no.62)

I saw a man arguing with the leader saying, why do you people separate religion from politics and you say 'there are no politics in the religion' although the religion contains aspects of politics?

The leader remained silent and did not give an answer as is their habit.

I saw a young man smoking at the door of the *Masjid* and he had a beautiful beard. I advised him to quit smoking and I gave him a hat [*Kufi*] as a gift. He put it on his head threw the cigarette on the ground. The leader found out about this and he summoned me. He rebuked it and said to me, leave him [alone] and let him smoke in the room next to the *Masjid* until he [automatically quits and] leaves it by himself!

I said, this is a huge mistake to leave him to smoke even if it is in the room next to the *Masjid*. The Messenger (صلى الله عليه وسلم) said,

"Whoever amongst you sees an evil should change it with the help of his hand; and if he has not able to, then [he should change it] with his tongue, and if he has not able to, then [he should abhor it] with his heart, and that is the least of *Īmān*."

(Reported by Muslim)[69]

We were passing through the market of (Hama) and one of the acquaintances said, I do not want to pass through this market because my father will see me and get angry since I left him alone in the shop. I left my wife alone at home and she is about to give birth.

So I said to him, this is not permissible according to *Sharī'ah*. Go to your father and apologise to him or send him a message. Go to your wife and enquire about how she is because she may be ill or need someone to take care of her and her children. Indeed the Messenger of *Allāh* (صلى الله عليه وسلم) said,

"It is enough as a sin for a person that he does not take care of those who rely upon him."

(*Hassan* reported by Ahmad and others)[70]

3. Then we went to Damascus and entered the *Kafr Sousah Masjid*. After the *Ṣalāh* a young man delivered a speech, in which he mentioned a *Ḥadīth* where he said, the world is a resting place for him who does not find any resting place.

After he finished his speech I said to him, is this *Ḥadīth Ṣahīh*? He said to me, I heard it from the friends [*Tablīghī Jam'āt*].

I said to him, this is not [sufficient] enough [as evidence]. He turned to a man that was a scholar next to him and asked him about the *Ḥadīth*. The scholar said to him, this is not a *Ḥadīth*.

Then I advised him in a very compassionate manner to find [and choose] the *Ṣahīh Aḥadīth* and stay away from the weak and fabricated *Aḥadīth*. When their leader saw me he came to me and he said to me, do not teach him, *Allāh* will teach him!!

Note that he dedicates lessons for them in Fiqh and other matters. Years passed by and I came to *Makkah*. I saw a man going to the *Haram* before the *Jum'ah Ṣalāh*. I caught up with him and greeted him

---

69 [TN] *Ṣaḥīḥ Muslim Ḥadīth* no.49

70 [TN] *Musnad Aḥmad Ḥadīth* no.6495, *Ṣaḥīḥ Muslim Ḥadīth* no.996

with *Salām*. I said to him, are you Abu Shakir [?]

He said to me, yes.

I said to him, you are the one who was in Damascus and you said to me, 'do not teach this young man, *Allāh* will teach him'

He said, yes.

I said, how can you say that whilst the Messenger of *Allāh* (صلى الله عليه وسلم) said,

"Knowledge is [acquired] by learning."

(*Hassan* see *Ṣahīh al-Jami*)[71]

He said to me, I made a mistake.

I advised him not to reject knowledge and advice. [Especially] Knowing that he is a teacher at *Ta'if* so he must have been educated [and acquired knowledge] in order to become a teacher.

I went on a journey with them [*Tablīghī Jam'āt*] and there were 3 of us. We entered a room where young men were playing cards and they call it *Ash-Shidda*. [The cards] contained pictures, numbers and quantities. I spoke in a very compassionate and soft manner to the young men and I said to them, this is impermissible and wastes your time. It will gradually lead you to gambling and creates enmity between the players.

They became convinced [accepted the advice] and began to tear the cards they were playing with. They gave me some of them so that I could join them in tearing them apart. So I tore up some of the cards and shared an earning of the reward together with them. Then they went with us for *Ṣalāh* in the *Masjid* and when their leader found out about that [card tearing incident] he summoned me. He rebuked me for tearing the cards that they were playing with. I said to him, they requested me to participate in the tearing, so I did. They are the ones who started tearing the cards before me.

[However] he did not accept that! I thought to myself, these people enjoin good and do not forbid evil whilst the Messenger of *Allāh* (صلى الله عليه وسلم) said,

'Whoever amongst you sees an evil should change it with the help of his hand; and if he has not able to, then [he should change it] with his tongue, and if he has not able to, then [he should abhor it] with his

---

[71] [TN] *Silsilah as-Sahībah Ḥadīth* no.342

heart, and that is the least of *Īmān*.'"

(Reported by Muslim)[72]

4. Then I went with them to Jordan and they have a big *Masjid* in (Amman) where they gather at. We went to the *Masjid* and we prayed *Ṣalāh* in it. Then one of the spokespersons gave a lecture in which he mentioned strange things. He said addressing those present, our beloved friends do not eat too much so you do not defecate a lot. *Imām* al-Ghazali went to *Ḥajj* for a month and did not defecate [i.e. he did not go to the toilet].

One of those who were sitting [in the audience] said to him, where did you get this story from?

So he rejected it [i.e accepting such an absurd story] from him because a person cannot stay [alive] for a month without relieving himself. Then the man got up and left the gathering from the *Masjid*.

Then he said in his lecture while reading from a book [called] *Life of The Companions*, when the Messenger (صلى الله عليه وسلم) returned from *Ta'if*, he met a servant named [Addas]. The Messenger of *Allāh* (صلى الله عليه وسلم) asked him about his [home town and] country? So he said, [I am] from the town of Nineveh.

He (صلى الله عليه وسلم) said to him, "From the town of Yūnus *('Alayhisalām)*, that is my brother in Prophethood."

So Addas prostrated to the Messenger (صلى الله عليه وسلم).

I was surprised by this speech. How can the Messenger (صلى الله عليه وسلم) be pleased with Addas prostrating to him? Whilst prostration is not permissible except for *Allāh*. This story is not *Ṣahīh*.

The *Ṣahīh* [incident and version of this story] is that Addas knelt at the feet of the Messenger (صلى الله عليه وسلم) kissing them. This kissing is completely different from prostration. So the book *Life of The Companions* is in need of verification in order to know [and distinguish] the *Ṣahīh* [narrations] from the *Da'īf* and fabricated ones.[73]

---

[72] [TN] *Ṣaḥīḥ Muslim Ḥadīth* no.49

[73] [TN] Some *Sūfīs* make a false interpretation in order to justify making prostration of respect to other than Allāh. They say that if the prostration is towards the elder and the intention is towards *Allāh* then there is no problem. One of them stated that, "...Just as in prostration to the *Ka'bah* [means] the one being prostrated to is

I advised and requested the brother Muhammad Ali Dawlah to verify the book because he was the one who printed and published it. He said to me, the whole book is about virtues and there are no *Sharī'ah* rulings in it.

I said to him, this is not true.

I showed him [as an example] of a *Ḥadīth* that was mentioned by the author of *Life of the Companions* which is, my companions are like the stars whichever of them you follow, you will be guided.

The scholars of *Ḥadīth* said about it that it is fabricated so the brother Muhammad Ali Dawla remained silent. I met with Shaykh Nayef Al-Abbasi, may *Allāh* the Most High have mercy on him, at Damascus and I said to him, I have read in the book *Life of the Companions* which is verified by you [in Arabic] with the following [comments], when the Messenger (ﷺ) returned from *Ta'if* and he (ﷺ) called them to *Islām*. They rejected his call and mistreated him, so he sat saying,

'O *Allāh*, I complain to You of the weakness of my strength, my lack of ability and my weakness towards people. To whom do you leave me? To an enemy who treats me harshly [?] or to a relative whom You have given ownership over my matter [?]. If you are not angry with me, then I do not care…' to the end of the *Dū'ā*.'

How can the Messenger (ﷺ) say admonishing his *Rabb*,

'To whom do you leave me?!' [i.e. leave me to]

Whilst *Allāh* the Most High said to him,

"Your *Rabb* has not taken leave of you, [O Muhammad], nor has He detested [you]."

(Surah Duha Āyah no.3)

[i.e. Your *Rabb* has neither forsaken you nor is angry with you.]

(See *Tafsīr Ibn Kathīr*)[74]

---

the *Haq* [*Allāh*] and the *Ka'bah* is the direction of the prostration." (*Bawadar an-Nawadar* by Ashraf Alī Thanvī p.128)

Other *Sūfīs* also are of the same view by stating that, "The one who prostrates to other than *Allāh* is not a disbeliever." (*Al-Mubayan* by Aḥmad Raza Khan p.70)

[74] [TN] *Tafsīr Ibn Kathīr* vol.8, p.425. Additionally the meaning is that, 'He has not

Shaykh Nayef Al-Abbasi said to me, by *Allāh* your words are correct. The Messenger of *Allāh* (صلى الله عليه وسلم) did not say this. However, I verified the book from the historical and linguistic point of view. This book needs someone like Shaykh Nasirudīn al-Albānī to reference check [and verify] it's *Aḥadīth.*

I said to him, indeed Shaykh Nasir [al-Albānī], may *Allāh* preserve him, had confirmed the *Ḥadīth* to be *Da'īf* and said, there is an unacceptable mistake in its text'.

Perhaps he [Shaykh al-Albānī] is referring to the statement,

'To whom do you leave me'.

Which contradicts the *Qur'ān* and the actuality."[75]

5. I attended a meeting of theirs in which their leader (Sa'īd al-Aḥmad) delivered a sermon and he said, the Messenger (صلى الله عليه وسلم) passed by a building, and he (صلى الله عليه وسلم) said to his companions, 'Whose [building] is this?'. They said, 'Of so and so [person]'. When the owner of the building passed by the Messenger (صلى الله عليه وسلم) he greeted him (صلى الله عليه وسلم) with *Salām*, [however] he (صلى الله عليه وسلم) did not respond to the owner of the building. The Companions *(Radī Allāhū 'Anhum)* informed the owner of the building about the reason, so the Companion *(Radī Allāhū 'Anhu)* went and demolished the building so that he (صلى الله عليه وسلم) would return his greetings of *Salām* him.

I say, that this *Ḥadīth* is not authentic because the Messenger (صلى الله عليه وسلم) said,

"Sound [legitimately acquired] wealth is very excellent for a

---

abandoned you since He has always taken care of you, nor has He neglected you since He raised and cared for you.' See *Tafsīr as-Sa'di* vol.10, p.411

[75] [TN] The tragedy is that those who have been caught in the *Da'wah* based on the stories of the *Tablīghī Jam'āt*, then sadly there is very little hope that they will return to the teachings of the *Qur'ān* and *Sunnah* and reform themselves because of their prejudice. It has happened that scholars of the religion point out some weaknesses in the *Tablīghī* curriculum with great sympathy and sincerity. However a storm arises from the *Tablīghī* circles and advertisements are made against it. The extremity of the *Tablīghī Jam'āt* is such that in places like India sometimes when there is an *Ahlul Ḥadīth Masjid* being built they demolish it and set fire to the workers house and vehicle.

righteous man!"[76]

(*Ṣahīh*, reported by *Aḥmad*)[77]

[76] [TN] The righteous man is the one who takes his money from a lawful way and spends it on charitable causes. Additionally if wealth is obtained in a legitimate way, it is a valuable blessing of *Allāh* and His special grace.

[77] [TN] *Ṣaḥīḥ al-Adab al-Mufrad Ḥadīth* no.299 by Shaykh Albānī

A DISCUSSION ABOUT THE CONDITIONS OF THE [*TABLĪGHĪ*] *JAM'ĀT*

Realisation [and verification] of the statement that [There is no deity except *Allāh* and Muḥammad is the Messenger of *Allāh*]. Indeed realisation [and verification] means understanding and implementation. So did this group understand the meaning of this pure statement which is the 1st pillar from the pillars of *Islām* contained in the *Ḥadīth* of Jibrīl *('Alayhisalām)* that was reported by [*Imām*] Muslim? Additionally, did they call for its implementation and acting upon it?

The reality is that they do not know its true meaning, which is, There is no deity worthy of worship in truth except *Allāh*, and Muḥammad is the preacher of the religion of *Allāh* which He is pleased with.

The evidence for this definition are the words of *Allāh* the Most High,

"That is because *Allāh* is the True Reality, and that which they call upon other than Him is falsehood, and because *Allāh* is the Most High, the Grand."

(Surah Ḥajj Āyah no.62)

If they knew its meaning they would call to it before anything else because it calls towards *Tawhīd* of *Allāh* and supplicating to Him alone and no one else. This is because of the statement of the Messenger (صلى الله عليه وسلم),

"*Dū'ā* is worship…"

(Reported by *at-Tirmidḥī* and he said it is *Hasan Ṣahīh*)[78]

Just as *Ṣalāh* is the worship of *Allāh* and it is not permissible [to be done] for a Messenger or a *Walī* then similarly *Dū'ā* is an act of worship and it is not permissible to ask from the Messengers or from the *Awlīyā*. I did not hear from the *Tablīghī Jam'āt* calling towards

[78] [TN] *Sunan at-Tirmidḥī Ḥadīth* no.2969 and *Ṣaḥīḥ ul-Jami' Ḥadīth* no.3407

understanding it and acting upon it.[79]

The one who supplicates to other than *Allāh* falls into the polytheism that abolishes the actions based on the statement of *Allāh* the Most High,

"And do not invoke [worship] besides *Allāh* that which neither benefits you nor harms you, for if you did, then indeed you would be of the wrongdoers."

[Meaning the polytheists]

(Surah Yunus Āyah no.106)

2. Establishing the *Ṣalāh* with reverence and humility.

Establishing the *Ṣalāh* means knowing its conditions, obligations, pillars and whatsoever rulings are related it, for example such as the prostration of forgetfulness. In accordance to what was mentioned in the *Ḥadīth*,

"Pray as you have seen me praying."

(Reported by *Bukhārī)*[80]

Did the *Tablīghī Jam'āt* teach these matters to their group? Also, did they explain to their group that humility in *Ṣalāh* means keeping one's thoughts [and concerns] on the recitation and glorifications [of *Allāh*] and not exaggerating movement during *Ṣalāh* and other important actions?

3. Knowledge with *Ḍhikr.*

This condition, like the rest of the conditions, was not fulfilled by the *Tablīghī Jam'āt.* I mentioned previously that I advised one of the youth who gave a lecture in which he mentioned a fabricated *Ḥadīth.* So their leader said to me, leave him. Do not teach him, *Allāh* will

---

79 [TN] What has been seen observed is that in the *Tablīghī Jam'āt* the words of elders, *Imāms* and *Awlīyā* are considered as the final word. On the other hand, *Ṣahīh Aḥadīth* which contain no room for ambiguity are rejected by making excuses and false interpretations.

80 [TN] *Ṣaḥīḥ Bukhārī Ḥadīth* no.6008

teach him!

Although the Messenger (ﷺ) said,

"Knowledge is [acquired] by learning."

(Hassan see *Ṣahīh ul-Jāmi'*)[81]

A delegation of them from Jordan visited me and I explained to them the *Aqīdah* of *Tawhīd* including the *Aqīdah* that *Allāh* is in the Heavens, as He informed of Himself in the statement of *Allāh* the most High,

"Do you feel secure that He who is above would not cause the earth to swallow you…"

(Surah Mulk Āyah no.16)

Ibn Abbas said,

"[He who is above] He is *Allāh* the Most High."[82]

I mentioned to them the *Ḥadīth* of the slave girl in which the Messenger (ﷺ) asked her, "Where is *Allāh*?'

She said, 'In the Heavens'

He (ﷺ) said, 'Who am I?'

She said, 'You are the Messenger of *Allāh* (ﷺ)'

He (ﷺ) said to her owner, 'Set her free for indeed she is a believer.'"

(Reported by *Muslim*)[83]

Those present were impressed by this information and they asked me for some booklets of knowledge, bearing in mind that many of them do not want to read books of knowledge. I gifted 2 of them some booklets to take with them and read it with their *Tablīghī Jam'āt* but they did not take it. It was from his (ﷺ) guidance that he

81 [TN] *Silsilah as-Sahīhah Ḥadīth* no.342

82 [TN] [Namely] He is Allāh the Most High, [who is] the Most High [far above] over His creation. *Tafsīr as-Sa'di* vol.10, p.170

83 [TN] *Sunan Abū Dāwūd Ḥadīth* no.3282 declared *Ṣaḥīḥ* by Shaykh Albānī

(صلى الله عليه وسلم) used to accept gifts. The Messenger (صلى الله عليه وسلم) said,

"Give each other gifts and you will love one another."

(Hassan, see *Ṣaḥīḥ ul-Jāmi'*)[84]

4. Honouring the Muslims.

The reality is that they honour their guests especially during mealtimes. They also talk a lot about honouring scholars, if only they took their advice and accepted their teachings. I travelled with them in many countries but they never allowed me to talk to them.

Rather, they allow 1 person from their group, even if he is ignorant, to speak to people and this does more harm than good. So they bring false *Aḥadīth* as was recently mentioned a previously and they bring a *Ḥadīth* which is not proven during eating and they say, speak during the meal even if it is related to the price of your weapons.

4. Sincerity of intention for *Allāh* the Most High.

It is an important condition and according to some of them it is necessary and obligatory. They go with the intention of preaching and spend from their wealth. The place of sincerity is the heart and no one knows it except for *Allāh*. Their individuals often speak about their preaching especially the leaders among them that such and such incident happened, they did such and such, their number was such and such [i.e. a lot] and many people accepted their preaching.

I ask *Allāh* that they be sincere in their work, however it is very important to have knowledge for sincerity in order for its individual to benefit from it and the *Ummah* also benefit from it.

Al-Bukhārī, may *Allāh* have mercy on him, mentioned in his book [a chapter heading entitled] 'The Chapter: Knowledge is Before Speech and Actions'. For this he has taken evidence from the words of *Allāh* the Most High,

"So know, [O Muḥammad], that there is no deity [worthy of worship in truth] except *Allāh*."

(Surah Muḥammad Āyah no.19)

---

[84] [TN] *Ṣaḥīḥ ul-Jāmi' Ḥadīth* no.3004

I have already mentioned that the brethren [*Tablīghī Jam'āt*], may *Allāh* guide them, do not care about [seeking] knowledge.

5. Preaching towards *Allāh*.

This is a good principle. It is obligatory for every Muslim to give importance to it in accordance to their capability. However calling to *Allāh* has an important condition that *Allāh* the Most High explained by His statement,

"Say, 'This is my way; I invite to *Allāh* with insight, I and those who follow me. And exalted is *Allāh*; and I am not of those who associate others with Him.'"

(Surah Yūsuf Āyah no.108)

[*Allāh*] the Most High is saying to His Messenger (ﷺ) and ordering him to inform the Jinn and Humankind that this is His way, path, method and practice. Which is to preach and call to testify that there is no deity worthy of worship in truth except *Allāh* alone who has no partners. To call to *Allāh* with insight, certainty and proof. He (ﷺ) and everyone who follows him (ﷺ) calls for what the Messenger of *Allāh* (ﷺ) called to with insight, certainty as well as rational and divine legislative proofs.

(Exalted is *Allāh*)[85] i.e. I glorify Him, exalt Him, revere Him and sanctify Him [and consider Him too holy] from having a partner or a rival, or someone like Him, or an equal, or a child, or parent, or wife, or minister, or deputy. He is Sanctified, holy and far above all of that.

(See *Tafsīr Ibn Kathīr* vol.2, p.495)

85 [TN] Explaining the words in *Sūrah Yūsuf Āyah no.108*

SUMMARY

While these are the conditions [which contain some form of structure] albeit inconsistent, nevertheless the group is deficient in the practical application of these conditions. Particularly in the matter of knowledge and substantiating the word [and components] of *Tawhīd* and calling to it before anything else in accordance with following the example of the Messenger of *Allāh* (صلى الله عليه وسلم) who stayed in *Makkah* for 13 years calling the people to it whilst enduring harm in the way of it.

However he (صلى الله عليه وسلم) was patient until *Allāh* helped him. The Arabs know the meaning of *Tawhīd* in the expression [There is deity except *Allāh*] thus they did not accept it because it invites them to worship *Allāh* [alone] and supplicate to Him alone as well as to leave supplicating others, even if they were from the Awlīyā and righteous people. *Allāh* the Most High said about the polytheists,

"Indeed they, when it was said to them, 'There is no deity but *Allāh*,' were arrogant and were saying, 'Are we to leave our gods for a mad poet?' Rather, he [i.e., the Prophet (صلى الله عليه وسلم)] has come with the truth and confirmed the [previous] messengers."

(Surat Saffat Āyah no.36)

THE RELIGION IS SINCERITY AND ADVICE

The Messenger of *Allāh* (صلى الله عليه وسلم) said,

"The Religion is sincerity [and advice]."

We said, 'To whom?'

He (صلى الله عليه وسلم) said,

"To *Allāh*, to His Book, To His Messenger, and to the leaders of the Muslims and to the common Muslim people."

(Reported by Muslim)[86]

Implementing on the words of this noble Messenger of *Allāh* (صلى الله عليه وسلم), I direct my advice to all the *Islāmic* groups to adhere to what came in the *Qur'ān* and the authentic ahadīth according to the understanding of the righteous predecessors, may *Allāh* be pleased with them, such as the companions and those that followed them, the *Mujtahid Imāms* and those who follow their path.

[86] [TN] *Ṣaḥīḥ Muslim Ḥadīth* no.103

THE *SŪFĪ* GROUPS

My advice to the *Sūfīs* is that they single out *Allāh* alone in supplications and seeking help, in accordance with the words of *Allāh* the Most High,

"It is You [alone] we worship and You [alone] we ask for help."

(Sūrah Fatiha Āyah no.5)

Additionally, the statement of the Messenger of *Allāh* (صلى الله عليه وسلم),
"*Dū'ā* is worship..."

(Reported by *at-Tirmidhī* and he said it is *Hasan Ṣaḥīḥ*)[87]

They should also believe that *Allāh* is above the heavens, according to the words of *Allāh* the Most High,

"Do you feel secure that He who is above would not cause the earth to swallow you..."

(Surah Mulk Āyah no.16)

Ibn Abbas said,
"[He who is above] He is *Allāh* the Most High."[88]

[Ibn ul-Jawzi mentioned it in his *Tafsīr*][89]

He (صلى الله عليه وسلم) said,
"...Will you not trust me, whereas I am a trustee of Him Who is above the heavens..."

(Agreed Upon)[90]

---

[87] [TN] *Sunan at-Tirmidhī Ḥadīth* no.2969 and *Ṣaḥīḥ ul-Jami' Ḥadīth* no.3407

[88] [TN] [Namely] He is Allāh the Most High, [who is] the Most High [far above] over His creation. *Tafsīr as-Sa'di* vol.10, p.170

[89] [TN] *Zād ul-Maysir Fī Ilm it-Tafsīr* vol.13 p.243

(The meaning of in [*Fī*] the heavens is: i.e. above [*'Ala*] the heavens)

2. They must limit their [method] of *Ḍhikr* only to what is mentioned in the *Qur'ān* and *Sunnah* and observe the practice of the Companions.

3. They should not give preference to the sayings of their Shuyūkh over the sayings of *Allāh* and His Messenger (صلى الله عليه وسلم) in accordance with *Allāh's* statement,

"O you who have believed, do not put [yourselves] before *Allāh* and His Messenger."[91]

(Surah Hujurat Āyah no.1)

(Meaning do not precede in words or deeds over the saying of *Allāh* and His Messenger (صلى الله عليه وسلم))

[Mentioned by Ibn Kathīr][92]

4. They must worship *Allāh* [alone], supplicate to Him in fear of His fire and hoping for His Paradise in accordance with His, the most High, statement,

"...And invoke Him in fear and aspiration..."

(Surah A'raf Āyah no.56)

He (صلى الله عليه وسلم) said,
"I ask *Allāh* for paradise and seek His refuge from the fire [of Hell]."

(Reported by *Abū Dawud* with an *Ṣaḥīḥ* chain of narration)[93]

---

90 [TN] *Ṣaḥīḥ Bukhārī Ḥadīth* no.4351, *Ṣaḥīḥ Muslim Ḥadīth* no.1064

91 [TN] Rather, wait for instruction and follow the way of the Prophet (صلى الله عليه وسلم)

92 [TN] *Tafsīr Ibn Kathīr* vol.7, p.364

93 [TN] *Sunan Abū Dāwūd Ḥadīth* no.793 graded *Ṣaḥīḥ* by Shaykh Albānī

5. The *Sūfīs* must believe that the first human being that was created is Ādam *('Alayhisalām)* and that Muhammad (صلى الله عليه وسلم) is a descendant of Ādam *('Alayhisalām)*. Additionally, all the people [humankind] are from his progeny and *Allāh* created them all from soil. *Allāh* the most High said,

"It is He who created you from dust, then from a sperm-drop…"

(Surah Ghafir Āyah no.67)

There is no [*Ṣaḥīḥ*] evidence that *Allāh* created Muḥammad (صلى الله عليه وسلم) from His light. What is known is that he (صلى الله عليه وسلم) was born from 2 parents.

JAMʾĀT AD-DA'WAH WAT-TABLĪGH [94]

1. My advice to them is that they adhere to what is stated in the Book [*Qurʾān*] and the authentic *Sunnah* in their *Daʾwah*. Additionally, that they learn the *Qurʾān*, Tafsīr and ḥadīth so that their *Daʾwah* is based upon knowledge, in accordance to the statement of *Allāh* the Most High,

"Say, 'This is my way; I invite to *Allāh* with insight..."

(Surah Yusuf Āyah no.108)

The saying of the Messenger (صلى الله عليه وسلم),
"Knowledge is [acquired] by learning."

(*Hassan* see *Ṣahīh al-Jami*)[95]

2. They adhere to the authentic ahadīth and they should avoid weak and fabricated ahadīth lest they come under the saying of the Messenger (صلى الله عليه وسلم),
"It is enough of a lie for a man to narrate everything he hears."

(Reported by Muslim)[96]

3. The people [*Tablīghī Jamʾāt*] should not separate enjoining good from forbidding evil because *Allāh* the Most High combined them in many āyāt such as the statement of *Allāh* the Most High,

"And let there be [arising] from you a nation inviting to [all that is] good, enjoining what is right and forbidding what is wrong [according to the laws of *Allāh*] and those will be the successful."

(Surah Āal Imran Āyah no.104)

---

94 [TN] Referring to the *Tablīghī Jamʾāt*

95 [TN] *Silsilah as-Sahīhah Ḥadīth* no.342

96 [TN] *Ṣaḥīḥ Muslim Ḥadīth* no.5

This is [something which] the Messenger of *Allāh* (صلى الله عليه وسلم) was concerned about and he (صلى الله عليه وسلم) commanded the Muslims to change [and eradicate] the evil. So he (صلى الله عليه وسلم) said,

"Whoever among you sees an evil, should change it with his hand, and if he does not have the ability to do that, then [he should change it] with his tongue, and if he does not have the ability to do that, then [he should detest it] with his heart, and that is the least of Iman.)

(Reported by *Muslim*)[97]

4. That they must concentrate on calling towards *Tawhīd* and give it priority over everything else in accordance with his (صلى الله عليه وسلم) saying,

"So let the very 1st thing to which you should call them to be the testimony that none has the right to be worshipped in truth except *Allāh* alone…"

(Agreed Upon)[98]

In [another narration the words are],

"…towards [accepting] the *Tawhīd* of *Allāh*…"

(Reported by *Bukhārī*)[99]

The *Tawhīd* of *Allāh* means singling Him out for acts of worship, especially in *Dū'ā* due to his Sal saying,

"*Dū'ā* is worship…"

(Reported by *at-Tirmidḥī* and he said it is *Hasan Ṣaḥīḥ*)[100]

---

97 [TN] *Ṣaḥīḥ Muslim Ḥadīth* no.49

98 [TN] *Ṣaḥīḥ Bukhārī Ḥadīth* no.1458 and *Ṣaḥīḥ Muslim Ḥadīth* no.19

99]TN] *Ṣaḥīḥ Bukhārī Ḥadīth* no.7372

100 [TN] *Sunan at-Tirmidḥī Ḥadīth* no.2969 and *Ṣahīh ul-Jāmi' Ḥadīth* no.3407

JAM'ĀT AL-IKHWĀN WAL-MUSLIMĪN[101]

1. That they should teach the members of their group about all the different forms of *Tawhīd* such as, *Tawhīd ar-Rabb*, *Tawhīd al-Ilāh* and *Tawhīd al-Asmā Was-Ṣifāt*. This is because it is very important on which the happiness [and success] of the individual and groups depends on instead of drowning in [worldly] politics and false truths. This does not mean [completely] ignoring [and not knowing] the conditions of the country and the people, but rather to not be excessive or have imprecision.
2. To stay away from *Sūfī* ideas that contradict the creed of *Islām*, since we have seen many of them mentioning false *Sūfī* doctrines in their books:
   a. Umar at-Tilmasani, who is their leader in Egypt, has a book entitled '*Shahid ul-Mihrab*' [*The Martyr Of The Mihrab*] which contains dangerous beliefs of *Sūfism* in it as well as [endorsing the] teaching of music.
   b. [Similarly] Syed Qutb has mentioned about *Wahdatul Wujūd*[102] in accordance to *Sūfism* which is in his book '*In The Shade Of The Qur'ān*'. He mentioned it at the beginning of *Surah al-Hadid* as well as other false interpretations. I spoke to his brother Muhammad Qutb to comment on [and correct] the mistakes related to creed given that he supervises [and is the editor] of the publication of '*Ash-Shuruq*'. So he refused and he said, my brother bears the responsible [for that].
   I was encouraged to review it by Shaykh Abdul Latif Badr, who is the supervisor of the magazine entitled '*At-Taw'iyah*' [Outreach].

---

101 [TN] Also known in English as the Muslim Brotherhood, it was founded by Hasan al-Bana in Egypt. Later on the likes of Syed Qutb provided it with intellectual foundations. This group arose with the slogan of the implementation of *Islām* but then jumped into the field of politics. They opposed the rulers and the struggle for power forced them to make *Takfīr* of the rulers. Thus they went so far as to become a *Takfīrī* group. To gain power they adopted democratic methods however when unsuccessful they finally armed themselves against the rulers. This group has mainly split into 2 factions. These people are very much influenced by the modern atheistic civilisation and they consider *Islamic* methods and the Sunnah as unnecessary.

102 [TN] The belief that *Allāh* actually exists everywhere in everything.

c. Sa'id Hawa mentions beliefs of the *Sūfīs* in his book *'Our Spiritual Training'*. They were mentioned at the beginning of the book.
d. Similarly, Shaykh Muhammad Hamid from Syria gifted me a book entitled, *'Rudud Ala Abatil'* [*Refutation Of Falsehoods*]. It contains good topics such as the prohibition of smoking etc. except that he has mentioned in it that there are *Abdāl*, *Aqtāb* and *Aghwāth*. However the *Gawth* is not called a *Gawth* except when someone is [making *Dū'ā* to and] seeking relief from him!!!
Seeking relief from [and supplicating to] the *Aghwāth* and Aqtāb is from the *Shirk* which destroys [and nullifies] deeds. It is from the *Sūfī* ideologies that are false which Islam rejects.
I requested from his son 'Abdurahmān to comment on his father's speech [written in the book which contains such false ideas] but he refused to do that.

3. That they do not hold a grudge against their *Salafī* brothers who call towards *Tawhīd*, fight against *Biḍ'ah* and resort to making decisions based on the *Kitāb* and *Sunnah*. They are their brothers. *Allāh* the Most High says,

"The believers are but one brotherhood..."

(Surah Hujurat Āyah no.10)

He (صلى الله عليه وسلم) said,
"None of you [truly] believes until he loves for his [Muslim] brother that which he loves for himself."

(Agreed Upon)[103]

[103] [TN] *Ṣaḥīḥ Bukhārī Ḥadīth* no.13 and *Ṣaḥīḥ Muslim Ḥadīth* no.45

THE *SALAFĪS* AND THE *ANSĀR AS-SUNNAH AL-MUHAMADIYAH*

1. My advice to them is that they [consistently] continue in their call towards *Tawhīd* and ruling by what *Allāh* has revealed as well as other important matters.
2. That they be gentle in their *Da'wah* and that they use soft words [and gentleness in their speech], regardless of the opponent in accordance with the statement of *Allāh* the Most High,

"Invite [all] to the Way of your Lord with wisdom and kind advice, and only debate with them in the best manner..."

(Surah Nahl Āyah no.125)

His, Most High, statement to Mūsā *('Alayhisalām)* and Hārūn *('Alayhisalām)*,

"Go, both of you, to Pharaoh, for he has truly transgressed [all bounds]. Speak to him gently, so perhaps he may be mindful [of Me] or fearful [of My punishment]."

(Surah Ṭahā Āyah no.43, no.44)

The statement of the Messenger of *Allāh* (صلى الله عليه وسلم),
"He who is deprived of gentleness is deprived of all goodness."

(Reported by Muslim)[104]

3. That they be patient with whatsoever harm they face, for indeed *Allāh* is with them through His help and support. *Allāh* the Most High says,

104 [TN] *Ṣaḥīḥ Muslim Ḥadīth* no.2592

"Be patient [O Prophet], for your patience is only with Allah's help. Do not grieve over those [who disbelieve], nor be distressed by their schemes. Surely *Allāh* is with those who shun evil and who do good [deeds]."

The statement of the Prophet (صلى الله عليه وسلم),

"The believer who mixes with people and endures [with patience] their harm is better than the one who does not mix with them and does not endure [with patience] their harm."

(*Ṣaḥīḥ*, reported by *Aḥmad* and other than him)[105]

4. That the *Salafīs* should not pay attention to the opponents that say your number is small, because *Allāh* the Most High says,

"...[Only] a few of My servants are [truly] grateful."

(Surah Saba Āyah no.13)

The Messenger of *Allāh* (صلى الله عليه وسلم) said,

"Glad tidings to the strangers." It was asked, 'Who are they, O Messenger of *Allāh* (صلى الله عليه وسلم)? He (صلى الله عليه وسلم) replied, "They are a small group of righteous people among a large evil population. Those who oppose them are more than those who follow them."

(*Ṣaḥīḥ*, reported by *Aḥmad* and *Ibn ul-Mubarak*)[106]

---

105 [TN] *Musnad Aḥmad Ḥadīth* no.5022, *Sunan Ibn Mājah Ḥadīth* no.4032 and *Ṣahīh ul-Jāmi' Ḥadīth* no.6651. The *Ḥadīth* is an indication of the virtue of patience, pardoning injustices and suppressing anger. These qualities only occur with those who mix with people since different people vary in their character and temperaments. These qualities rarely occur in a person if he does not mix with other people. Mingling with people is a way to spread good morals and virtues through influencing them.

106 [TN] *Musnad Aḥmad Ḥadīth* no.6650, *Musnad 'Abdullāh b. al-Mubarak Ḥadīth* no.23, *Ṣahīh ul-Jāmi' Ḥadīth* no.3921 and *Silsilah as-Sahīhah Ḥadīth* no.1273

HIZB UT-TAHRĪR

1. My advice to them is to apply the teachings of Islam to themselves before they request others to apply it. About 20 years ago 2 young men from them visited me in Syria. Their beards were [clean] shaved and the smell of [cigarette] smoke was coming from them. They asked me to join them in a discussion. So I said to them, you shave your beards and smoke [cigarettes], although these 2 are *Ḥarām* in the *Sharī'ah.* Then you also consider it permissible to shake hands with women, whereas the Messenger of *Allāh* (صلى الله عليه وسلم) said,

"For one of you to be pierced in the head with an iron needle is better for him than to touch a woman that is not permissible for him."

(*Ṣaḥīḥ*, reported by *at-Ṭabarānī*)[107]

They said to me, it was mentioned in al-*Bukhārī* that the Messenger (صلى الله عليه وسلم) used to shake hands with women during the pledge of allegiance!!

So I said to them, tomorrow you will bring me the *Ḥadīth.* So they left and did not return therefore I knew that they were lying and that al-*Bukhārī* never mentioned that. Rather he only mentioned the pledge of allegiance to women without shaking hands.

What is strange is that some of the *Ikhwān ul-Muslimīn* permit shaking hands with women, such as [what is mentioned in the books of] Shaykh Muhammad al-Ghazali and Yusuf al-Qardawi. Based on a discussion that took place between me and between him, he cited as evidence the *Ḥadīth* of the slave girl who took the hand of the Messenger (صلى الله عليه وسلم)in order [that he (صلى الله عليه وسلم)take her so that she is able] to meet her needs.

(Reported by *Bukhārī*)[108]

---

[107] [TN] *Silsilah as-Sahīhah Ḥadīth* no.226, *Al-Mu'jam Al-Kabīr of Ṭabarānī Ḥadīth* no.16910,

[108] [TN] *Ṣaḥīḥ Bukhārī Ḥadīth* no.6072 and *Sunan Ibn Mājah Ḥadīth* no.4177. Meaning that the humility and character of the Messenger of *Allāh* (صلى الله عليه وسلم) was at

I say, indeed his reasoning is incorrect bearing in mind that when the slave girl took his (صلى الله عليه وسلم) hand she did not touch it, but rather touched the sleeve of his (صلى الله عليه وسلم) shirt which was on his (صلى الله عليه وسلم) hand. This is because Aisha *(Radī Allāhū 'Anha)* said,

"...No, by *Allāh*, his (صلى الله عليه وسلم) hand never touched a lady's hand to pledge allegiance. They did not pledge their allegiance [to him (صلى الله عليه وسلم)] except by saying, 'Indeed I have accepted your pledge of allegiance for that.'"

(Reported by *Bukhārī*)[109]

He (صلى الله عليه وسلم) said,

"Indeed I do not shake hands with women."

(Reported by *at-Tirmidhī* and he said it is *Hasan Ṣaḥīḥ*)[110]

2. I heard a sermon from a Shaykh who is affiliated to *Hizb ut-Tahrīr* in Jordan in which he was criticizing the rulers who rule by other than what *Allāh* revealed. When I went to his house his father in-law complained and said indeed the Shaykh hit his wife on her eye and affected her! So I said to the Shaykh, you demand the implementation of the *Sharī'ah* from the rulers whilst you did not enforce the *Sharī'ah* in your own house. Is it true that you hit your wife on her eye [?]. So he said, yes however it was a light hit with a cup of tea!

So I said to him, implement *Islām* on yourself 1st then request others to implement it. The Messenger (صلى الله عليه وسلم) was asked what is the right of the wife of one of us over him? He (صلى الله عليه وسلم) replied,

"That you should give her food when you eat, clothe her when

---

such a level that if anyone had a need he (صلى الله عليه وسلم) would go with them and help fulfil it. He (صلى الله عليه وسلم) would not have neglected the person's request until he (صلى الله عليه وسلم) assisted them. This also shows the prominence of the Prophet (صلى الله عليه وسلم) to the people and his (صلى الله عليه وسلم) closeness to them.

109 [TN] *Ṣaḥīḥ Bukhārī Ḥadīth* no.4891

110 [TN] *Ṣahīh ul-Jāmi' Ḥadīth* no.2513 and *Silsilah as-Sahīhah Ḥadīth* no.529

you clothe yourself, do not hit her on the face, do not insult her[111] nor separate yourself from her except in the house."

(*Ṣaḥīḥ*, reported by the 4)[112]

He (ﷺ) said,

"When one of you strikes his servant, then he should avoid striking the face."

(*Hasan* reported by *Abū Dāwūd*)[113]

---

111 [TN] *Imām* Abū Dāwūd said, [the meaning of] do not insult her is that you say [for example] may *Allāh* make you ugly. See *Sunan Abū Dāwūd Ḥadīth* no.2142

112 [TN] *Ṣaḥīḥ Sunan Abū Dāwūd Ḥadīth* no.2142

113 [TN] *Ṣahīh ul-Jāmi' Ḥadīth* no.674, *Sunan Abū Dāwūd Ḥadīth* no.4493

JAM'ĀT UL-JIHĀD AND OTHERS

1. My advice to them is that they be gentle in their *Da'wah* and their *Jīhād* especially to the rulers in accordance to the statement of *Allāh* the Most High to Musa *('Alayhisalām)* when He sent him *('Alayhisalām)* to Pharaoh the disbeliever,

"[Commanding] "Go to Pharaoh, for he has truly transgressed [all bounds]. And say, 'Would you [be willing to] purify yourself."

(Surah Nazi'at Āyah no.17, 18)

The statement of Him the Most High,

"Go, both of you, to Pharaoh, for he has truly transgressed [all bounds]. Speak to him gently, so perhaps he may be mindful [of Me] or fearful [of My punishment]."

(Surah Taha Āyah no.43, no.44)

The statement of his (صلى الله عليه وسلم),
"He who is deprived of gentleness is deprived of all goodness."

(Reported by *Muslim*)[114]

2. Advice to the Muslims leaders and rulers consists of helping them on the truth and obeying them in it as well as instructing them [with good] and prohibiting them [from evil] and admonishing them with gentleness. Refraining from rebelling against them with the sword if there appears to be unfairness [injustice] or ill-treatment on their part.

(See the statement of al-Khaṭābī in the commentary of 40 *Ḥadīth*)

The author of *Aqīdah at-Ṭaḥawīyah* (Abū Ja'far at-Tahāwī) said,

---

[114] [TN] *Ṣaḥīḥ Muslim Ḥadīth* no.2592

"We do not believe in revolt against our leaders and rulers, even if they commit injustice, nor do we make *Dū'ā* against them or withdraw our obedience from them. We see the obedience to them is a part of our obedience to *Allāh*, so long as they do not order anything sinful. We pray for them to be righteous and for their well-being."[115]

Allāh the Most High says,

"O believers! Obey *Allāh* and obey the Messenger and those in authority among you…"

(Surah Nisa Āyah no.59)

3. The Messenger of *Allāh* (صلى الله عليه وسلم) said,

"Whoever obeys me, then he has indeed obeyed *Allāh*, and whoever disobeys me, then indeed he has disobeyed *Allāh*. Whoever obeys the ruler, then he has indeed obeyed me, and whoever disobeys the ruler, then he has indeed disobeyed me."

(Reported by *Bukhārī* and *Muslim*)[116]

4. From Abū Dhar *(Radī Allāhū 'Anhu)* that he said,

"My close friend [the Prophet (صلى الله عليه وسلم)] advised me to hear and obey [the ruler] even if he is a maimed slave…"

(Reported by *Muslim*)[117]

5. He (صلى الله عليه وسلم) said,

"It is [obligatory upon] a Muslim that he should listen [to the ruler appointed over him] and obey him whether he likes it or not, except that he is ordered to do a sinful thing. If he is ordered to do a sinful act, then [a Muslim should] neither listen to him nor should he obey [his orders]."

(Agreed Upon)[118]

---

[115] [TN] *Matn Al-Aqīdah At-Ṭaḥawīyah* p.24

[116] [TN] *Ṣaḥīḥ Bukhārī Ḥadīth* no.7137 and *Ṣaḥīḥ Muslim Ḥadīth* no.1835

[117] [TN] *Ṣaḥīḥ Muslim Ḥadīth* no.648

6. From Hudhaifah b. al-Yaman *(Radī Allāhū 'Anhu)* that he said,

"The people used to ask the Messenger of *Allāh* (صلى الله عليه وسلم) about the good, but I used to ask him about the bad fearing lest it overtake me. I said, O Messenger of *Allāh* (صلى الله عليه وسلم) indeed we were in the midst of ignorance and evil, and then *Allāh* brought us this good [through *Islām*]. Is there any evil after this good? He (صلى الله عليه وسلم) said, "Yes." So I asked, will there be a good [again] after that evil? He (صلى الله عليه وسلم) said, "Yes, but there is a smoky taint in it [i.e. a smokescreen]." I asked, what will be the smoky taint in it [i.e. a smokescreen]? He (صلى الله عليه وسلم) said, "The people who will adopt ways other than my *Sunnah* and seek guidance other than mine. There will be good and bad in them." I asked, will there be evil after that good? He (صلى الله عليه وسلم) said, "Yes people inviting at the gates of Hell and whosoever responds to their call will be thrown into it." I said, O Messenger of *Allāh* (صلى الله عليه وسلم), describe them for us. He (صلى الله عليه وسلم) said, "All right they will be a people having the same complexion [appearance and race] as ours and speaking our language." I said, O Messenger of *Allāh* (صلى الله عليه وسلم), what do you suggest [and advise] if that period reaches me? He (صلى الله عليه وسلم) said, "You should stick to the main body of the Muslims and their leader." I said, [what] if they have no main body [of Muslims] and have no leader? He (صلى الله عليه وسلم) said, "Separate yourself from all of these sects even if [that means] you may have to bite [and eat] the roots of trees until death comes to you and you are on that [condition]."

(Agreed Upon)[119]

7. The Messenger of *Allāh* (صلى الله عليه وسلم) said,

"Whosoever sees something from his leader that he disapproves of then he should be patient. For indeed he who separated from the main body of the Muslims even to the extent of a hand span and then dies, he will die as those who died in the Pre-*Islāmic* period of ignorance."

---

118 [TN] *Ṣaḥīḥ Bukhārī Ḥadīth* no.7144 and *Ṣaḥīḥ Muslim Ḥadīth* no.1839

119 [TN] *Ṣaḥīḥ Bukhārī Ḥadīth* no.3606 and *Ṣaḥīḥ Muslim Ḥadīth* no.1847

(Agreed Upon)[120]

8. He (صلى الله عليه وسلم) said,

"The best of your rulers are those whom you love and who love you, who invoke *Allāh's* blessings upon you and you invoke His blessings upon them. The worst of your rulers are those whom you hate and who hate you and whom you curse and they curse you. We said, O Messenger of *Allāh* (صلى الله عليه وسلم) shouldn't we overthrow them with the help of the sword during that [time]. He (صلى الله عليه وسلم) said, no as long as they establish the Salah among you. Indeed one who has a governor appointed over him and he sees him committing things that are disobedient to *Allāh* he should dislike their committing of disobedience to *Allāh* and do not withdraw yourselves from their obedience."

(Reported by Muslim)[121]

9. The Book and the *Sunnah* indicate the necessity of obeying those in authority, unless they order disobedience. So consider the saying of *Allāh* the Most High,

"O believers! Obey *Allāh* and obey the Messenger and those in authority among you..."

(Surah Nisa Āyah no.59)

[However, there is a point to be considered here and that is] how He says,

"...and obey the Messenger..."

He did not say and obey those in authority from among you because those in authority are not singled out for obedience [as the benchmark]. Rather they are obeyed [provided that their obedience is] in [accordance with] the obedience of *Allāh* and His Messenger (صلى الله عليه وسلم). He repeated the verb [of obedience] with the Messenger

120 [TN] *Ṣaḥīḥ Bukhārī Ḥadīth* no.7143 and *Ṣaḥīḥ Muslim Ḥadīth* no.1849

121 [TN] *Ṣaḥīḥ Muslim Ḥadīth* no.1855

(صلى الله عليه وسلم) because whosoever obeys the Messenger (صلى الله عليه وسلم) then he has indeed obeyed *Allāh*. So this is since indeed the Messenger (صلى الله عليه وسلم) does not command anything other than obedience to *Allāh*. Rather he (صلى الله عليه وسلم) is infallible in this regard. As for the one in authority then indeed he may command [something] other than obedience to *Allāh* so he is not obeyed except in what is obedience to *Allāh* and His Messenger (صلى الله عليه وسلم).

As for obeying them even if they are unjust then that is because abandoning their obedience results in a lot more evils than what occurs from their injustice. Rather being patient with their injustice becomes a means of expiation for sins and multiplication of rewards. For *Allāh* has not given them power over us except due to the corruption of our deeds and the recompense is based on the nature of the deed. So it is upon us that we seek forgiveness, repent and reform our deeds. *Allāh* the Most High says,

"Whatever affliction befalls you is because of what your own hands have committed. And He pardons much."

(Surah Shura *Āyah* no.30)

He the Most High says,

"This is how We make the wrongdoers [destructive] allies of one another because of their misdeeds."
(Surah An'ām Āyah no.129)

If the subjects [who are being ruled] want to be freed from the oppression of the oppressive ruler then they should leave oppression themselves.

(See *Sharh Aqīdah at-Ṭaḥawīyah* p.380, 381)

10. *Jihād* against the Muslim rulers is to offer advice to them and their helpers according to the statement of the Messenger of *Allāh* (صلى الله عليه وسلم),

"The Religion is sincerity." We said, to whom? He (صلى الله عليه وسلم) said, "To *Allāh*, to His Book, to His Messenger, and to the leaders of the

Muslims and their general people."

(Reported by Muslim)[122]

Additionally due to his (صلى الله عليه وسلم) statement,

"The best *Jihād* is [to speak] a word of justice to an oppressive ruler."

(A *Hasan Ḥadīth* reported by *Abū Dāwūd* and *Tirmidhi*)[123]

The explanation for the way to be saved from the oppression of the rulers who are from our complexion [appearance and race] and speak our language is that the Muslims repent to their *Rabb*, correct their beliefs and educate themselves as well as their families upon the correct *Islām* in fulfillment of the words of *Allāh* the Most High,

"...*Allāh* would never change a people's state [of favour] until they change their own state ˹of faith˺..."

(Surah Ra'd Āyah no.11)

One of the modern-day preachers pointed this out by saying, establish the rule of *Islām* in your hearts and *Allāh* will grant you rule on Earth.

Similarly, it is necessary to reform the foundation of the government and that foundation is the society. *Allāh* the Most High says,

"*Allāh* has promised those of you who believe and do good that He will certainly make them successors in the land, as He did with those before them; and will surely establish for them their faith which He has chosen for them; and will indeed change their fear into security—˹provided that˺ they worship Me, associating nothing with Me. But whoever disbelieves after this ˹promise˺, it is they who will be the rebellious."

122 [TN] *Ṣaḥīḥ Muslim Ḥadīth* no.55

123 [TN] *Ṣaḥīḥ at-Targhīb Wat-Tarhīb Ḥadīth* no.2305 and *Sunan Abū Dāwūd Ḥadīth* no.4344. This is because one's life is at immediate risk.

(Surah Nūr Āyah no.55)

(Summarised from the book which has notes on the explanation of *At-Ṭaḥawīyah* by Shaykh Albānī)

MY ADVICE TO ALL THE GROUPS

I have reached a very old age and I am now nearly 70 years old. I would like good for all groups in accordance with the general statement by the Messenger (ﷺ) that,

"The Religion is sincerity [and advice]…"

(Reported by Muslim)[124]

So I offer the following advice:

To adhere to the *Qur'ān* and the *Sunnah* of the Prophet (ﷺ), in accordance with the statement of *Allāh* the Most High,

"And hold firmly together to the rope of *Allāh* and do not be divided…"

(Surah Āal-Imran Āyah no.103)

His (ﷺ) statement,

"I am leaving you with 2 things that you will not go astray as long as you adhere to them. [One of them is] the Book of *Allāh* and [the other is] the *Sunnah* of His Messenger (ﷺ)."

(Reported by *Mālik* and declared *Ṣahīh* by Shaykh al-Albānī in *Ṣahīh ul-Jāmi'*)[125]

When the groups disagree [with each other] then they must refer to the *Qur'ān*, the *Ḥadīth* and the practice of the Companions *(Radī Allāhū 'Anhu)*
in accordance with the statement of *Allāh* the Most High,

"…Should you disagree on anything, then refer it to *Allāh* and His Messenger, if you ⌜truly⌝ believe in *Allāh* and the Last Day. This is the best and fairest resolution."

---

124 [TN] *Ṣaḥīḥ Muslim Ḥadīth* no.103

125 [TN] *Muwatta Imām Mālik Ḥadīth* no.1598 and *Ṣahīh ul-Jāmi' Ḥadīth* no.2068

(Surah Nisā Āyah no.59)

The statement of the Messenger (صلى الله عليه وسلم),

"…It is [obligatory] upon you to adhere to my *Sunnah* and the *Sunnah* of the rightly guided caliphs…"

(*Ṣahīh* reported by Ahmad)[126]

That they pay attention to the belief of *Tawhīd* which the *Qur'ān* emphasised on and the Messenger (صلى الله عليه وسلم) started his call to it, and ordered his companions to start with it.

I have interacted with [many] *Islāmic* groups, and I saw that the *Salafī Da'wah* adheres to the Book and the *Sunnah* according to the understanding of the righteous predecessors, [such as] the Messenger (صلى الله عليه وسلم), his (صلى الله عليه وسلم) companions and the *Tabi'īn*. The Messenger (صلى الله عليه وسلم) referred to this group by saying,

"Beware! The people of the Book before you were split up into 72 sects, and this Ummah will be split into 73 sects, 72 of them will go to Hell and 1 of them will go to Paradise, and it is the mainstream group [i.e. those who follow the *Qur'ān* and *Sunnah*]."

(Reported by Ahmad and al-Hafiḍh [Ibn Ḥajar declared it] *Hasan*)[127]

In another narration [which has additional words],

"All of them will be in the fire except 1, [i.e. those who are on] what I and my companions are upon."

(Reported by *Tirmidḥī* and declared *Hasan* by Shaykh al-Albānī)[128]

The Messenger (صلى الله عليه وسلم) informed us that the Jews and Christians are greatly divided [into many sects] and that the Muslims will be divided more than them. That all these sects will be vulnerable to entering Hell, due to their deviation and distance from the Book of their *Rabb*

---

126 [TN] *Ṣahīh ul-Jāmi' Ḥadīth* no.2549

127 [TN] *Ṣaḥīḥ at-Targhīb Ḥadīth* no.51

128 [TN] *Ṣahīh ul-Jāmi' Ḥadīth* no.5343 and *Sunan at-Tirmidḥī Ḥadīth* no.2641

and the *Sunnah* of their Prophet (ﷺ). That only 1 sect will be saved from Hell and enter Paradise. That is the group that adheres to the *Qur'ān* and the *Sunnah* and the practice of the Companions *(Radī Allāhū 'Anhu).*

The *Salafī* call is distinguished by its call to *Tawhīd* and battling *Shirk*. [As well as having] knowledge of the authentic Ahadith [along with] warning against the weak and fabricated Ahadith. Having knowledge of the *Sharī'ah* rulings with their evidences and this is very important for every Muslim [to know].

I advise my Muslim brothers to adhere to the *Salafī Da'wah* because it is the saved sect and the victorious group about which the Messenger (ﷺ) said,

"There will never cease to be a group from my Ummah manifest upon the truth. Those who oppose them will not be able to harm them until Allah's command is executed [i.e. the Day of Judgement is established]."

(Reported by Muslim)[129]

O *Allāh* make use from the saved sect and the victorious group. [Amin]

129 [TN] *Ṣaḥīḥ Muslim Ḥadīth* no.1920

IN CONCLUSION

1. It is necessary for all the *Islāmic* groups to stay away from partisanship that harbours hatred and that leads to division. They must cooperate with each other in what benefits the Muslims and brings them good and prosperity according to the statement of *Allāh* the Most High,

"...cooperate with one another in goodness and righteousness, and do not cooperate in sin and transgression..."

(Surah Mā'idah Āyah no.2)

The statement of the Messenger (صلى الله عليه وسلم),

"...be as servants of *Allāh* and brothers. A Muslim is the brother of a Muslim. He neither oppresses him nor humiliates him nor looks down upon him. The piety is here, [and while saying so] he pointed towards his chest. It is a serious evil for a Muslim that he should look down upon his brother Muslim. All things of a Muslim are inviolable for his brother Muslim [such as] his blood, his wealth and his honour..."

(Reported by Muslim)[130]

2. It is necessary for all the *Islāmic* groups to not have jealousy of each other nor hold grudges as per his (صلى الله عليه وسلم) statement,

"...do not be jealous of each other, do not hate each other and do not desert each other..."

(Reported by Muslim)[131]

3. Every *Islāmic* group must accept advice when it is in accordance with the *Qur'ān* and *Ṣahīh Aḥadīth* as per his (صلى الله عليه وسلم) statement,
"The Religion is sincerity [and advice]..."

---

[130] [TN] *Ṣahīh ul-Jāmi' Ḥadīth* no.7242 and *Ṣaḥīḥ Muslim Ḥadīth* no.2564

[131] [TN] *Ṣaḥīḥ Muslim Ḥadīth* no.2563

(Reported by Muslim)[132]

His (صلى الله عليه وسلم) statement,

"All of the children of Adam sin, and the best of those who sin are the ones who repent."

(*Hasan* reported by Ahmad and other than him)[133]

I conclude my speech with the following *Dū'ā*,

O *Allāh*, resolve [peace] between us, join our hearts and guide us to the path of safety. O *Allāh* make us guided and [from] those who lead the way of guidance, and not from those who are misguided nor those who misguide others. [Make us] be at peace with your *Awlīyā* and at war with your enemies. May *Allāh's* blessings and greetings of peace be upon Muhammad, his family [and those who follow him].

---

132 [TN] *Ṣaḥīḥ Muslim Ḥadīth* no.103

133 [TN] *Ṣahīh ul-Jāmi' Ḥadīth* no.4515, *Sunan Ibn Mājah Ḥadīth* no.4251, *Musnad Aḥmad Ḥadīth* no.13049

WARNINGS ON OBSERVATIONS

Allāh the Most High has blessed me and I began to call towards *Tawhīd* of *Allāh* the Most High. I published more than 20 books, each of which was printed numerous times in large quantities. Some of them have been translated into languages such as English, French, Indonesian, Urdu, Bengali and Turkish etc. Most of these books were printed with the help of donors and it is distributed free of charge. Some of it is sold in the bookshops that print at their own expense. Indeed I have written the following phrase on each book [that],

Every Muslim has the right to print and translate [these books] and whosoever has any feedback on the books then please inform the author [about it].

I received a book from the Arab Emirates entitled '*The Beliefs Of Al-Imām Al-Hafiḍh Ibn Kathīr*' by the author Muhammad Adil Azizah. When I read it I found that he did not adhere to scholarly integrity, even in the Prophetic *Aḥadīth*, where he removed the *Ḥadīth* which was mentioned by Ibn Kathīr during the commentary of the statement of *Allāh* the Most High,

"[Beware of]` the Day the Shin will be disclosed."

(Surah Qalam Āyah no.42)

This is what the Messenger (صلى الله عليه وسلم) said [regarding it],

"Our *Rabb* will disclose His Shin, and then all the Believers, men and women, will prostrate themselves before Him…"

To the end of the *Ḥadīth* which was reported by *Bukhārī* and Muslim.[134]

He said in his book,

Muhammad Jamīl Zeno fumbled a lot in his book (*The Methodology Of The Saved Sect*) on p.16 and elsewhere.

Allāh knows that I was happy and I said [to myself] perhaps I

---

134 [TN] *Ṣaḥīḥ Bukhārī Ḥadīth* no.4919

made a mistake and so I will rectify my mistake.

When I looked in my aforementioned book I found the following, (*Imām* Ahmad said, *Imām* Shafi'ī said, *Imām* Khatīb Baghdādī said)

So I called the author and I said to him, what is the blunder which I mentioned in my book?
So he said to me, I don't have the book with me.

So I said to him, why did you remove the *Ḥadīth* which explains the *Āyah* from *Tafsīr* Ibn Kathīr?

So he said to me, the *Ḥadīth* is from the *Mutashābihāt!!*[135]
I said to him, why did you remove the statement of Ibn Kathīr in explanation of,

"He is [the Only True] *Allāh* in the heavens..."

(Surah An'ām Āyah no.3)

Where he selected the statement of the *Mufassir* at-Tabarī to prove that *Allāh* is in heaven?

So he said to me, wait until I look.

[In the end] He did not acknowledge his mistake.

I refuted this author in a book entitled *'A Clarification And Warning From The Book The Beliefs of Al-Imam al-Hafiḍh Ibn Kathīr'*.

I read in a book entitled *'In The Prophetic School'* by brother Ahmad Muhammad Jamal in which he said, I was surprised by brother (Muhammad Jamīl Zeno) when he wrote in the *An-Nadwa* newspaper on the 26/4/1411 Hijri denouncing the format of blessings upon the Messenger (صلى الله عليه وسلم) which some Muslims are used to reciting. It is their saying [of],

---

[135] [TN] Meaning those *Āyāt* which require further explanation and are not always entirely clear to everyone. Although the whole *Qur'ān* is entirely clear for those who have the knowledge of its correct intended meanings such as the scholars of the *Qur'ān*.

O *Allāh* send blessings upon, the remedy and healing of hearts, and the well-being and cure of bodies, and the light and radiance of the eyes.

He [then] said, indeed the healer and bringer of well-being of the bodies, hearts and eyes is *Allāh* alone. The Messenger (صلى الله عليه وسلم) does not possess the ability to benefit himself or anyone else etc. I would like brother Muhammad Zeno to know that this format has 2 correct concepts,

a. Indeed the remedy of the hearts and the well-being of bodies as well as the light of the eyes are an attribute or a fruit [of benefit] of sending blessings upon the Messenger (صلى الله عليه وسلم). We have known from the previous Ahadith the virtue of sending blessings upon the Messenger (صلى الله عليه وسلم) and its subsequent blessings and that it emanates from *Allāh* Almighty…
The blessings of *Allāh* upon his servants is the mercy, blessing, well-being and healing.

b. Indeed the remedy of the heats, the well-being of the bodies and the light of the eyes are attributes of the Messenger (صلى الله عليه وسلم) himself…there is no denying this and nor is there abnormality in it since the Messenger (صلى الله عليه وسلم) essence, as described in the noble Qur'an, is a mercy in the statement of *Allāh* the Most High,

"We have not sent you except only as a mercy for the whole world."

(Surah Anbiya Āyah no.107)

He (صلى الله عليه وسلم) is also light and radiance as described in the *Qur'ān* in the statement of [*Allāh*] the Almighty,

"O Prophet! We have sent you as a witness, and a deliverer of good news, and a warner, and a caller to ⌜the Way of⌝ *Allāh* by His command, and a beacon of light."

(Surah *Ahzāb Āyah* no.45, 46)

In multiple reports the Messenger (صلى الله عليه وسلم) describes himself as a mercy that has been gifted to humanity to bring it out of darkness into light, heal the hearts, eyes and bodies from both physical and emotional ailments. He (صلى الله عليه وسلم) said,

"Indeed I am only a gifted mercy."

(Reported by *Ibn 'Asākir*)[136]

"Indeed I am a mercy that *Allāh* has sent."

(Reported by *at-Ṭabarānī*)[137]

"I have not been sent as the invoker of curse, but I have been sent as mercy."

(Reported by Muslim)[138]

I say, the previous format that the author said about which is used by people to recite is not permissible because sending blessings upon the Prophet (صلى الله عليه وسلم) is an act of worship.

Worship is based on waiting until evidence comes. There is no evidence for this format especially since it contradicts all of the narrations which were reported from the Messenger (صلى الله عليه وسلم), his

---

136 [TN] *Ṣahīh ul-Jāmi' Ḥadīth* no.2345 and *Silsilah as-Sahīhah Ḥadīth* no.490

137 [TN] *Mu'jam al-Kabīr of at-Ṭabarānī Ḥadīth* no.1532. The chain is not *Ṣaḥīḥ* for the wording of this *Ḥadīth* due to it containing a narrator called Aḥmad b. Ṣālih. However the wording of the *Ḥadīth* is similar to other *Ṣaḥīḥ Ahadīth* such as *Ṣahīh ul-Jāmi' Ḥadīth* no.2728 and *Ṣaḥīḥ Muslim Ḥadīth* no.2599. The weakness identified here is *Wijādah* (discovery) which means taking knowledge from a written source without hearing it, receiving permission to narrate it or transference of it. This comes under the category of *Munqati' and Mursal.* An example of *Wijādah* is when = a student comes across someone else's book in that individual's own handwriting containing some *Ḥadīth* which he relates and the student has never him, or he did meet him but did not hear the from him the *Ḥadīth* which he has found recorded in his handwriting and he does not have a license from him or anything similar. See *Mūqadimah Ibn Ṣalāh* p.125 under category no.24 point no.8 *Wijādah. Ahadīth* like this are not taken as an evidence by agreement of the scholars of *Ḥadīth*. See *Silsilah as-Sahīhah* vol.1, p.886

138 [TN] *Ṣaḥīḥ Muslim Ḥadīth* no.2599

companions *(Radī Allāhū 'Anhum)* and the pious predecessors. Additionally, it contains exaggeration and praise that *Allāh* and the Messenger (صلى الله عليه وسلم) do not approve of. So is it permissible for a Muslim to abandon the format that the Messenger (صلى الله عليه وسلم) taught his companions *(Radī Allāhū 'Anhum)* and adopt a format from what people say which contradicts the legislated format?

Indeed the author removed something important from my words which is my citation of Allah's statement,

"Say, "I have no power to benefit or protect myself, except by the Will of *Allāh*."

(Surah Ā'rāf Āyah no.188)

His (صلى الله عليه وسلم) statement,

"Do not exaggerate in praising me as the Christians praised the son of Mary, for I am only a Slave. So, call me the Slave of *Allāh* and His Apostle."

(Reported by *Bukhārī*)[139]

As for the author's statement, the blessings of *Allāh* upon His servants are mercy, blessings, well-being and healing. Ibn Kathīr said, the blessings from *Allāh* the Most High upon His servant are His praise amongst the Angels.

(*Tafsīr* Ibn Kathīr vol.3, p.495)

This is the correct *Tafsīr* which invalidates the *Tafsīr* of the author (Ahmad Muhammad Jamal) which there is no evidence for.

As for his using the statement of *Allāh* the Most High,

"We have not sent you except only as a mercy for the whole world."

(Surah Anbiya Āyah no.107)

---

139 [TN] *Ṣaḥīḥ Bukhārī Ḥadīth* no.3445 and *Ṣahīh ul-Jāmi' Ḥadīth* no.7363

So I will quote to the reader what the scholar Muhammad Amīn ash-Shinqītī said in his *Tafsīr* of it,

What *Allāh* Almighty mentioned in this *Āyah*, that he (ﷺ) was not sent except as a mercy to the Worlds indicates that he brought mercy to the creation as what is contained in this great *Qur'ān*. This meaning was demonstrated in [various] places in the Book of *Allāh* as per the statement of the Most High,

"Is it not enough for them that We have sent down to you the Book, [which is] recited to them. Surely in this [*Qur'ān*] is a mercy and reminder for people who believe."

(Surah Ankabūt Āyah no.51)

His statement the Most High,

"You never expected this Book to be revealed to you, but [it came] only [as] a mercy from your *Rabb*..."

(Surah Qasas Āyah no.86)

From Abu Hurayrah *(Radī Allāhū 'Anhu)* he said, it was to Allah's Messenger (ﷺ) invoke curse upon the polytheists, he (ﷺ) said,
"I have not been sent as the invoker of curse, but I have been sent as mercy."

(Reported by Muslim)[140]

(See *Adhwa ul-Bayan of Ash-Shinqītī* vol.4, p.694)

As for at-Tabarī he said, the summary of which is, *Allāh* sent Muhammad (ﷺ) as a mercy to all the Worlds both believers and unbelievers. As for the believers from them then indeed *Allāh* guided them through him (ﷺ) and admitted them into Paradise, through their belief in him (ﷺ) and what came from *Allāh*. As for the

---

140 [TN] *Ṣaḥīḥ Muslim Ḥadīth* no.2599

disbelievers from them he (صلى الله عليه وسلم) impeded the immediate calamity that used to befall the nations who denied their Messengers before him.

As for the statement of the author, he is (meaning the Messenger (صلى الله عليه وسلم)) light and radiance as described by the *Qur'ān* in the statement of His Almighty,

"O Prophet! We have sent you as a witness, and a deliverer of good news, and a warner, and a caller to [the Way of] *Allāh* by His command, and a beacon of light."

(Surah Ahzāb Āyah no.45, 46)

Then I will quote to the reader what the scholars of *Tafsīr* have said about it.

Ibn Kathīr said in his *Tafsīr*, O Prophet (صلى الله عليه وسلم), indeed we have sent you as a witness to your nation, bringing glad tidings of Paradise and warning against Hell. Calling towards the testimony that there is no deity that has the right to be worshipped in truth except *Allāh* alone by His permission and a beacon of light with the Qur'an.

So the statement of *Allāh* the Most High,

"…a witness…"

(Surah Ahzāb Āyah no.45)

Meaning [a witness] for *Allāh's* oneness and that there is no deity that has the right to be worshipped in truth other than Him. As well as [a witness] over the people and their actions on the day of Judgement.

"…bring you [O Prophet] as a witness against yours?"

(Surah Nisā Āyah no.41)

The statement of His Almighty,

"...and a deliverer of good news, and a warner..."
(Surah Ahzāb Āyah no.45)

Meaning a deliverer of glad tidings to the believers of abundant reward and a warner to the unbelievers of a distressing punishment.

His Greatness's statement,

"...and a caller to [the Way of] *Allāh* by His command..."

(Surah Ahzāb Āyah no.45)

Meaning a caller to the creation to worship their *Rabb* by His command to you to do so.

His, the Most High, statement,

"...and a beacon of light."

(Surah Ahzāb Āyah no.45)

Meaning your affair is as clear as the truth you have brought like the Sun in its radiance and illumination. It is not denied except by only the stubborn people.

(See Tafsīr Ibn Kathīr vol.3, p497)

Ibn ul-Jawzi said in his *Tafsīr Zād ul-Maysir*,

"...and a beacon of light."

(Surah Ahzāb Āyah no.45)

Meaning you are (a light) for those who follow you i.e. like a light that shines in the darkness by which it guides.

([*Zād ul-Maysir*] vol.6, p.400)

At-Tabarī said in his *Tafsīr*,

"…and a beacon of light."

(Surah Ahzāb Āyah no.45)

Illumination for His creation with the light you brought to them from Allah. Rather, what it means by this is that he (صلى الله عليه وسلم) guides those of his nation who follow him (صلى الله عليه وسلم).

(Summarised quote from at-Tabarī)

The author said in his book *'In the Prophetic School'*, in multiple narrations the Messenger (صلى الله عليه وسلم) describes himself as 'a gifted mercy' to the humankind to bring it out of darkness into light and to heal it's hearts and eyes from both physical and emotional ailments.

The Prophet (صلى الله عليه وسلم) said,
"Indeed I am only a gifted mercy."

(Reported by *Ibn 'Asākir*)[141]

"Indeed I am a mercy that *Allāh* has sent."

(Reported by *at-Ṭabarānī*)[142]

"I have not been sent as the invoker of curse, but I have been sent as mercy."

(Reported by Muslim)[143]

---

141 [TN] *Ṣahīh ul-Jāmi'* *Ḥadīth* no.2345 and *Silsilah as-Sahīhah* *Ḥadīth* no.490

142 [TN] *Mu'jam al-Kabīr of at-Ṭabarānī* *Ḥadīth* no.1532. The chain is not *Ṣaḥīḥ* for the wording of this *Ḥadīth* due to it containing a narrator called Aḥmad b. Ṣālih. For further details see footnote no.140

143 [TN] *Ṣaḥīḥ Muslim* *Ḥadīth* no.2599

I say, indeed the words of the author (Ahmad Muhammad Jamal) contain observations

a. The author did not provide evidence for his statement other than the *Ḥadīth* he cited,
   "Indeed I am only a gifted mercy."

[*Ṣahīh ul-Jāmi' Ḥadīth* no.2345]

The *Tafsīr* of mercy in the *Āyah* has been mentioned previously by *Allamah* Shinqītī and that the Messenger (صلى الله عليه وسلم) brought mercy to the creation as what is contained in this great *Qur'ān*.

b. As for the author's statement, to bring humanity out of darkness into light…

If only he referred to *Tafsīr* Ibn Kathir where he said about it,

"…so that you may lead people out of darkness and into light…"

(Surah Ibrahīm Āyah no.1)

Meaning We have only sent you, O Muhammad (صلى الله عليه وسلم), with this book to bring people out of the misguidance and sin that they are in to the guidance and right path. *Allāh* the Most High says,

"He is the One Who sends down clear revelations to His servant to bring you out of darkness and into light…"

(Surah Hadīd Āyah no.9)

The *Āyāt* are clear that he (صلى الله عليه وسلم) brought people of darkness into light with the *Qur'ān* which was revealed to him.

c. As for the author's statement, …heal the hearts, eyes and bodies from both physical and emotional ailments. He meant [by this] the Prophet (صلى الله عليه وسلم).

He did not provide clear evidence for that, knowing that the healer of diseases is *Allāh* alone. *Allāh* the Most High said on the tongue of *Ibrahīm ('Alayhisalām)*,

"And He [alone] heals me when I am sick."

(Surah Shu'ara Āyah no.80)

He emphasized the separate pronoun in order to emphasise that the healer is *Allāh* alone. The Messenger (صلى الله عليه وسلم) said,

"O *Allāh*, the *Rabb* of the people. Remove the problem and heal the patient, for You are the Healer. No healing is of any avail but Yours; healing that will leave behind no ailment."

(Reported by *Bukhārī*)[144]

The story of the boy and the blind man that was mentioned in the *Ḥadīth* proves that the healer is *Allāh* alone. It was mentioned in it that the blind man brought many gifts to the boy and said to him, 'I will give them all to you if you heal me'. So the boy said, indeed I do not heal anyone, only *Allāh* heals so if you believe in *Allāh* and I will make *Dū'ā* to *Allāh* so that He heals you. So he believed in *Allāh* so he made *Dū'ā* for him and consequently *Allāh* healed him.

(The story was reported by Muslim vol.4, *Ḥadīth* no.3005)[145]

So the previous *Āyah* and Ahadith prove that the healer is *Allāh* alone. The author (Ahmad Muhammad Jamal) did not mention a single example that the Messenger (صلى الله عليه وسلم) described himself (صلى الله عليه وسلم) as being a healer as he claimed. This is a very dangerous matter because he (صلى الله عليه وسلم) said,

"Whosoever says about me what I did not say, then let him take his eat in the Fire [of Hell]."

(*Hasan* reported by Ahmad)[146]

---

144 [TN] *Ṣaḥīḥ Bukhārī Ḥadīth* no.5743

145 [TN] *Ṣaḥīḥ Muslim Ḥadīth* no.3005

146 [TN] *Silsilah as-Sahīhah Ḥadīth* no.3100 and *Musnad Aḥmad Ḥadīth* no.469

I asked his eminence Shaykh Ibn Baz, the *Mufti* of Saudi Arabia, about the speech of (Ahmad Muhammad Jamal) and he responded, indeed it is *Shirk*.

AN IMPORTANT NOTICE

I say, indeed the Messenger (ﷺ) performed many miracles however they were during his (ﷺ) lifetime.

These are examples of them:

a. From Abdullah b. Mas'ūd *(Radī Allāhū 'Anhu)* he said, once we were with Allah's Messenger (ﷺ) on a journey, and we ran short of water. He (ﷺ) said,

"Bring the water remaining with you." The people brought a utensil containing a little water. He (ﷺ) placed his hand in it and said, "Come to the blessed water, and the blessing is from *Allāh*." I saw the water flowing from among the fingers of *Allāh*'s Messenger (ﷺ), and no doubt, we heard the meal glorifying *Allāh*, when it was being eaten (by him).

(Reported by *Bukhārī*)[147]

The Messenger (ﷺ) pointed out to his companions *(Radī Allāhū 'Anhu)* that the blessed water that flows from between his fingers is blessed by *Allāh* alone, who created this miracle. This is the Messenger's (ﷺ) keenness to guide his nation to *Tawhīd* and that is why he (ﷺ) said to them,

"...and the blessing is from *Allāh*."

b. There is Ali *(Radī Allāhū 'Anhu)* that came to the Messenger (ﷺ) and he was suffering from eye trouble. So The Messenger (ﷺ) put saliva on his eyes and made *Dū'ā* for him. Thus he was healed as if he had no ailment.

(Reported by *Bukhārī*)[148]

I say, these miracles occurred in his (ﷺ) lifetime and that the Messenger (ﷺ) made *Dū'ā* for Ali *(Radī Allāhū 'Anhu)* after putting

---

147 [TN] *Ṣaḥīḥ Bukhārī Ḥadīth* no.3579

148 [TN] *Ṣaḥīḥ Bukhārī Ḥadīth* no.2942

saliva on his eyes and he was healed. This is because the *Dū'ā* of the Prophet (صلى الله عليه وسلم) is answered. As for after his (صلى الله عليه وسلم) death the request for *Dū'ā* from him (صلى الله عليه وسلم) stopped and the miracles stopped as he (صلى الله عليه وسلم) said,

"When a man dies, his acts come to an end, but 3, recurring charity, or knowledge (by which people) benefit, or a pious child, who prays for him (for the deceased)."

(Reported by Muslim)[149]

There is Abū Ṭalib, the paternal uncle of the Messenger (صلى الله عليه وسلم), who used to defend him (صلى الله عليه وسلم). When he was near his deathbed the Messenger (صلى الله عليه وسلم) called him to *Imān* but he refused and he died as a polytheist. It was revealed about him,

"You surely cannot guide whoever you like ˹O Prophet˺, but it is *Allāh* Who guides whoever He wills…"

(Surah Qasas Āyah no.56)

(Reported by *Bukhārī*)[150]

[149] [TN] *Ṣaḥīḥ Muslim Ḥadīth* no.1631 and *Ṣahīh ul-Jāmi' Ḥadīth* no.793
[150] [TN] *Ṣaḥīḥ Bukhārī Ḥadīth* no.3884

THE *DŪʾĀ* AT NIGHT IS ACCEPTED

The Messenger (صلى الله عليه وسلم) said,

"Whoever gets up at night and says,

'La ilaha il-lallah Wahdahu la Sharika lahu Lahu-lmulk, waLahu-l-hamd wahuwa 'ala kullishai'in Qadir. Al hamdu lil-lahi wa subhanal-lahi wa la-ilaha il-lal-lah wa-l-lahu akbar wa la hawla Wala Quwata il-la-bil-lah.'

[None has the right to be worshipped in truth except *Allāh*. He is the Only One and has no partners. For Him is the Kingdom and all the praises are due for Him. He is Omnipotent. All the praises are for *Allāh*. All the glories are for *Allāh* and none has the right to be worshipped but *Allāh*, and *Allāh* is Great and there is neither Might nor Power Except with *Allāh*].

And then says, *Allahumma, Ighfir li* [O *Allāh*! Forgive me]. Or invokes (*Allāh*), he will be responded to and if he performs ablution (and prays), his prayer will be accepted."

(Reported by *Bukhārī*)[151]

([The meaning of the word] *Ta'ara* is to wake up)

I read this *Dūʾā* in order to recover from illnesses, and *Allāh* healed me. I read it in order to facilitate some tiring tasks, so *Allāh* gave me relief. I advise every Muslim to read this *Dūʾā* to solve all problems.

---

151 [TN] *Ṣaḥīḥ Bukhārī Ḥadīth* no.1154

IN CONCLUSION

Indeed the speech of the author (Ahmad Muhammad Jamal) has no evidence and it contains exaggeration and praise which the Messenger (صلى الله عليه وسلم) forbade by saying,
"...and beware of going to extremes in religious matters, for those who came before you were destroyed because of going to extremes in religious matters."

(*Ṣahīh*, reported by Ahmad)[152]

"Do not exaggerate in praising me as the Christians praised the son of Mary, for I am only a Slave. So, call me the Slave of *Allāh* and His Apostle."

(Reported by *Bukhārī*)[153]

Especially when the author claimed that the Messenger (صلى الله عليه وسلم) described himself (صلى الله عليه وسلم) as healing the hearts and eyes from both the physical and emotional ailments!

The word (to heal) is a present tense verb that refers to the present and the future and this is never possible. This healing has not happened in the present time nor in the future.

What I have mentioned in terms of the warnings regarding the book *'In the Prophetic School'* is from the approach of advice to the general Muslims and in particular for the readers of the aforementioned book.

I ask *Allāh* that He benefit the Muslims with it and make it purely for *Allāh* the Most High.

---

[152] [TN] *Musnad Aḥmad* Ḥadīth no.3248, *Ṣaḥīḥ Sunan Nasā'ī Ḥadīth* no.3057 and *Ṣahīh ul-Jāmi' Ḥadīth* no.2680

[153] [TN] *Ṣaḥīḥ Bukhārī Ḥadīth* no.3445 and *Ṣahīh ul-Jāmi' Ḥadīth* no.7363

Printed in Great Britain
by Amazon

41876445R00072